The
Institutes
of
Christian
Religion

JOHN
CALVIN

The
Institutes
of
Christian
Religion

*Edited by Tony Lane
and Hilary Osborne*

BAKER BOOK HOUSE
Grand Rapids, Michigan 49516

Reprinted 1987 by Baker Book House
from the edition ©1986 by
Robert Backhouse and published by
Hodder & Stoughton, London.
Used with permission

ISBN: 0-8010-2524-9

Printed in the United States of America

CONTENTS

PART III: GOD THE TRINITY AND HIS CREATION

PART IV: GOD'S PROVIDENCE

PART V: MAN'S SIN AND GOD'S REMEDY

**BOOK TWO
THE KNOWLEDGE OF GOD THE REDEEMER,
IN CHRIST.**

PART IX: THE CHRISTIAN LIFE

PART X: JUSTIFICATION BY FAITH

PART XI: PRAYER

PART XII: GOD'S ELECTION AND MAN'S DESTINY

PART XIII: THE CHURCH

BOOK FOUR
OUTWARD MEANS BY WHICH GOD HELPS US

PART XIV: THE SACRAMENTS

INTRODUCTION

Why should anyone today want to read Calvin's *Institutes*? To answer this question we need to see who Calvin was, how and why he wrote the *Institutes* and the purpose of this present edition.

John Calvin was born on July 10th, 1509, at Noyon in northern France. By the time that he had become a student at Paris, the Protestant Reformation was under way in Germany and the ripples were reaching Paris. Some time in the early 1530s, 'God by a sudden conversion subdued and brought my mind to a teachable frame,' as Calvin himself put it. His conversion was to the service of Jesus Christ and, in particular, to the Protestant cause. As a result, he had to leave France in 1534, because of a fierce campaign of persecution which was launched against the Protestants. Calvin withdrew to Basel, in Switzerland, where he hoped to lead the quiet life of a scholar and writer. But in August 1536 he was forced by circumstances to stop overnight at Geneva. William Farel, who had recently introduced the Reformation into Geneva, saw Calvin's potential and bullied him into staying as a Bible teacher.

Geneva was to remain Calvin's home, except for a period of exile from 1538 to 1541. This exile was caused at least in part by the youthful Calvin's excessive zeal, which had not yet been moderated by experience. Not that Calvin ever abandoned his zeal: on his return to Geneva he worked hard to transform the city into a godly society. For many years he faced intense opposition and at times it looked as if exile was again to be the order of the day. But eventually, owing to the mistakes of his opponents and to a considerable influx of French refugees (who supported Calvin), the pro-Calvin faction came to control the city council. Calvin never became the dictator of popular legend, but in the final years before his death in 1564 his goals for the city were increasingly realised. John Knox, the Scottish Reformer, who spent some time in the city, called it 'the most perfect school of Christ that ever was in the earth since the days of the apostles'.

Very early on, the Protestant movement divided into two groups. Martin Luther introduced the Reformation into Germany and from there it spread into Scandinavia and parts of Eastern Europe. At about the same time as Luther, and largely independently, Ulrich Zwingli was introducing the Reformation into Switzerland. This form of Protestantism came to be known as 'Reformed', as opposed to 'Lutheran'. It spread to Britain, France and Holland, as well as to parts of Germany and Eastern Europe. It was very similar to Lutheranism, but there were significant differences, especially concerning the nature of the sacraments. Zwingli died in 1531, while the movement was still relatively in its infancy. Calvin in due course became *the* leading theologian of Reformed Protestantism – which is, therefore, often known as 'Calvinism'. His *Institutes* constitutes the most important single work of Reformed theology ever written.

Calvin was a prolific writer. The *Institutes* is his best-known work, which he carefully revised a number of times. But in terms both of time devoted and of quantity produced, Calvin's major contribution lies in the area of biblical interpretation. He wrote commentaries on almost all of the New Testament and on much of the Old Testament. He preached about two hundred times a year for most of his time in Geneva. Many of his sermons survive, though unfortunately the majority have been lost. Calvin's many other writings include letters to a wide range of correspondents, 'church works' (such as liturgies, catechisms and confessions of faith) and theological treatises.

Calvin's *Institutes* is his most important work. The first edition was completed when he was only 26. It appeared in 1536, in a pocket-book format. It was short – about three-quarters of the length of the New Testament. It was primarily modelled on the traditional catechism, with chapters each on the Ten Commandments, the Apostles' Creed, the Lord's Prayer and the sacraments (baptism and the Lord's Supper). There were also two other chapters and a letter of dedication addressed to the king of France. Three years later the second edition appeared, nearly three times as long as the first. The additional material was written during Calvin's first stay in Geneva. While he was away from Geneva, in Strasburg, he worked on a further, less radical, revision which appeared in 1543. The next important revision was in 1550, when for the first time the chapters were subdivided into sections.

During the winter of 1558/9 Calvin lay ill with malaria and determined to produce a definitive edition of the *Institutes*. This appeared in September 1559. Calvin added much new material and this edition is nearly as long as the whole Bible. Calvin also thoroughly rearranged the book. He tells us that while he did not regret the earlier editions, he 'never felt satisfied until the work was arranged in the order in which it now appears'. There were eighty chapters, divided for the first time into four books, which correspond to the four sections of the Apostles' Creed. But this arrangement is largely formal and it would be wrong to see the work as an exposition of the Creed. The final resurrection comes at the end of Book 3, far from its position in the Creed.

References to the *Institutes* normally give the book, chapter and section. Thus 3:1:2 refers to Book 3, chapter 1, section 2. In this edition, each book and chapter begins with its number and with the title that Calvin himself gave it. Section numbers will be found at the beginning of each new section.

A French translation of the second (1539) edition appeared in 1541. From then on, all the major editions were translated into French. This was a major event in the history of the French language – the appearance in French of a major theological work. Calvin's elegant French style played an important formative role in the development of French as a modern language. These French editions show that Calvin was concerned to reach the lay people of France, not just the theologians and Latin-speaking intellectuals.

Why did Calvin write his *Institutes*? The first edition was meant to be a simple handbook on Christian doctrine – hence the pattern of a catechism. But by the time it was completed the king of France, Francis I, had unleashed a fierce campaign of repression against the French Protestants, branding them as seditious revolutionaries. Calvin thereupon wrote an introductory letter dedicating the volume to Francis, as a confession of faith and as an 'apology' (defence) for French Protestantism.

In the later editions another aim comes to the fore. The *Institutes* is intended as an introduction and guide to the study of the Bible. The *Institutes* is intended to complement Calvin's commentaries. He was concerned to keep his commentaries brief. Because of the *Institutes*, he did not need to digress at length on theological issues in his commentaries. Thus the *Institutes* and the commentaries are designed to be used together: the *Institutes* to provide a theological undergirding for the commentaries and the latter to provide a more solid explanation of the passages cited in the former.

But why read the *Institutes* today? There are several reasons. It is one of the most important theological works ever written and has had a profound influence upon European (and, indeed, world) history, secular as well as religious. Its influence has extended far beyond the circle of those who would think of themselves as 'Calvinists'. Again, it is one of the greatest theological works ever written.

Even after all these years, we can learn much from it, even if we are not 'Calvinists' and do not always agree with Calvin.

But to call the *Institutes* a *theological* work might be to give the wrong impression. The subtitle of the first edition is revealing: 'Embracing almost the whole sum of piety [or 'godliness'] and whatever is necessary to know the doctrine of salvation: A work most worthy to be read by all persons zealous for piety [or 'godliness'].' This was above all to be a practical book, to be a book about the Christian life. This concern is apparent throughout the work. Calvin abhorred and repeatedly attacked all useless speculation. He requires of all doctrine that it be scriptural and that it be useful for Christian living. This is most obviously true of the five chapters on the Christian life, but it is equally true of other chapters (like that on prayer) and it affects the way in which he discusses more theoretical doctrines like Providence or predestination. The second and longest of his three chapters on Providence is devoted to showing how we may use the doctrine for our benefit.

Why this new edition of the *Institutes*? There have been four complete English translations over the years. The first was made in Calvin's own lifetime (1561) by Thomas Norton, the son-in-law of the English Reformer Thomas Cranmer. In the last century there were two translations, by John Allen (1813) and Henry Beveridge (1845). The most recent was by F.L. Battles (1961). The last two are still in print. But few have the stamina to read the whole of the *Institutes*. Apart from the question of length (over 1,500 large pages in the Battles translation), there is much in the text that is of little interest to the reader today. And yet there is also a considerable amount of material that is as relevant today as on the day that it was written. (Some, indeed, more so, such as his warnings against the perils of materialism.) The aim of the present edition is to make this material accessible to the non-specialist reader. Two steps have been taken to this end. First, a selection has been made of the most important 15 per cent or so of the text. Second, this material has been rewritten in simpler and more modern English. The result is a selection from the *Institutes* which is manageable for the average modern reader, in terms of length and of intelligibility.

On what basis has the selection been made? This is an important question. Selections can seriously distort a writer's thoughts. The aim of the present selection has been to include the heart of Calvin's teaching on all his major themes. Chapters which are predominantly negative (like those attacking the Roman Catholic doctrines of penance or the mass, for instance) have been omitted. A major portion of the fourth book concerns the history of the early Church and the rise of the papacy. This has been omitted. Again, where Calvin expounds a particular doctrine, the aim is to select those passages where Calvin explains his own position, omitting passages where he engages in lengthy controversy with others, or where he amasses quotations from earlier writers to support his case. But even with these criteria, the constraint of length has forced some hard choices. Inevitably some will feel that their favourite passages have been omitted. I am sorry, but would assure them that there has been no deliberate bias. My aim has been simply to select the heart of Calvin's positive teaching – even on those points where I might not happen to agree with him.

Finally, to assist the modern reader, the text has been divided by themes into fourteen 'parts'. These might have been called chapters had not Calvin himself pre-empted this by his own use of the term. But in order not to distort Calvin's own layout, his own book and chapter headings are retained.

A Note on this Edition

Calvin wrote the *Institutes* in Latin. Henry Beveridge translated it into an English closely based on the Latin in the last century, and his work has formed the basis of the present translation into modern English, reference being made to the original Latin where problems have arisen.

Where a whole chapter or section of Calvin's text has been omitted in the present version, this has been indicated by putting the section or chapter number in square brackets: [3–4] means sections 3 and 4 have been omitted and [ch 15] indicates a chapter has been omitted. Within a section, where a significant amount of text is omitted, this is marked with dots thus … , but these have not always been used where it is only a sentence or two that has been omitted, or where a section is paraphrased.

Passages from the Bible are generally quoted from the New International Version, published by Hodder & Stoughton, but where this does not reflect Calvin's use of the Latin text alterations have been made to the NIV so as to avoid confusion in understanding Calvin's thought. Bible references are almost entirely Calvin's own; a few have been inserted for the reader's convenience by the present editor, but only where Calvin unambiguously quotes or refers to particular passages.

[*Tony Lane* conducted research on Calvin under the internationally respected Calvin scholar T.H.L. Parker at Cambridge, and is collaborating on the first English translation of Calvin's work on The Bondage of the Will. Since 1973 he has taught Christian doctrine to undergraduate and postgraduate students at the London Bible College, where he offers a special course on Calvin's *Institutes*. He is the author of *The Lion Concise Book of Christian Thought* as well as of a number of articles on Calvin. Tony Lane is married with two daughters, aged 6 and 4.]

Part I

KNOWING GOD AND OURSELVES

BOOK ONE

THE KNOWLEDGE OF GOD THE CREATOR

Chapter 1

The link between knowledge of God and ourselves and the nature of it.

1. Our wisdom, if it is to be thought genuine, consists almost entirely of two parts: the knowledge of God and of ourselves. As these are closely connected, it is not easy to decide which comes first and gives rise to the other. To begin with, no one can assess himself without turning his thoughts towards the God in whom he lives and moves, because it is quite obvious that the gifts we possess cannot possibly spring from ourselves and our very being is sustained by God alone. Further, the blessings which constantly spill over from heaven are like streams leading us to the fountain. Here again, the endless good which exists in God becomes more obvious beside our poverty. Most of all the sad ruin into which man's first rebellion plunged us compels us to turn our eyes upwards, not only that in our desperate need we may ask for what we want, but also that in fear we may learn humility. Because man is so full of misery and ever since the Fall has exhibited such a catalogue of blatant sin, everyone who is stung by the awareness of his own unhappiness gains at least some knowledge of God. So our

feelings of ignorance, vanity, need, weakness and general depravity remind us that in the Lord, and no one else, can be found the true light of wisdom, solid virtue and over-flowing goodness. Our evil ways make us think of all the good things of God. We can never really seek him in earnest until we begin to despair of ourselves. Don't we all rely on our own strength when we are not aware of our real nature and are quite content with our own gifts, ignoring our misery? When we do come to ourselves, we are spurred on to seek God and are led by his hand to find him.

2. On the other hand, it is evident that man never arrives at true self-knowledge before he has looked into the face of God and then come away to look at himself. For (such is our innate pride) we always seem to ourselves just and up-right, wise and holy until we are convinced, by clear proof, of our injustice and deviousness, stupidity and impurity. However, we are never convinced of this if we simply look to ourselves and not to the Lord as well, since he is the only yardstick from which this conviction can come. For since we all have a tendency to hypocrisy, any hollow appearance of righteousness is quite enough to satisfy us, instead of righteousness itself. Since there is nothing in us or around us that is not greatly tainted with impurity, as long as we are assessing limits of human corruption, anything which is slightly less putrid makes us very pleased with ourselves. It is like an eye which has never been shown anything other than black, assessing an object which is really off-white or discoloured, as pure white. To take this further: if, at mid-day, we look down at the ground or on any object which is lying around, we think our eyesight is strong and accurate. But when we look up at the sun and gaze at it with no pro-tection, the vision which was fine for the earth is so dazzled and confused by the brilliant sunlight that we have to admit that clear sight for earthly things is very dim when applied to heavenly. It is exactly the same when it comes to asses-sing our spiritual qualities. So long as we do not look

further than those around us, we are quite satisfied with our own righteousness, wisdom and virtue; we assess ourselves in very flattering terms as being well on the way to perfection! However, as soon as we lift our thoughts to God and reflect on his nature and how absolutely perfect he is in righteousness, wisdom and virtue, we realise that this is the standard to which we must conform. Then what previously made us very pleased by its deceptive outward goodness, we will see as tainted with the blackest sin; what before deceived us unbelievably, by masquerading as wisdom, will revolt us by its extreme folly; and what looked like commendable activity will be judged pathetic weakness. In just this way, even the qualities in us which seem most admirable are worlds away from God's purity and can never match it.

3. This explains the reverence and awe with which, as Scripture constantly tells us, holy men were struck whenever they became aware of the overwhelming presence of God. When we see those who were once so strong and confident, shaking with terror at the fear of death and completely devastated, we realise that men are never really convinced of their own insignificance until they contrast themselves with God's majesty. Frequent examples of such dismay occur both in the book of Judges and the prophetic writings, so that 'we shall die, for we have seen the Lord' was a common expression among God's people. So also the book of Job, in humbling men by convicting them of their foolishness, feebleness and sin, always makes its most important points by describing God's wisdom, virtue and purity. With good reason! We see Abraham much readier to humble himself the closer he got to seeing the glory of the Lord (Gen. 18:27), and Elijah unable to stand with his face uncovered as he approached, so awesome was the sight (1 Kgs 19:13). And what can man do, man who is rotten to the core and so wretched, when even the angels veil their faces in terror? It is to this undoubtedly that Isaiah refers when he says 'The moon will be abashed, the sun ashamed; for the Lord Al-

mighty will reign' (Isa. 24:23). When he shows forth his glory and gives a closer glimpse of it, the brightest objects will be covered in darkness by comparison (Isa. 2:10, 19). But though the knowledge of God and the knowledge of ourselves are bound together by a mutual bond, it is only right that the former is given first place, and then we can come down to the latter.

Chapter 2

What it is to know God and where that leads.

1. By the knowledge of God, I mean the way we not only understand that there is a God, but also grasp what this means to us personally, leading to our glorifying him: in short, what we really need to know about him. For we cannot say truthfully that God is known where there is no evidence in belief or practice. I am not referring here to the particular knowledge by which people, lost and condemned, lay hold of God as their redeemer, in Christ the Mediator. I speak of the simple and basic knowledge to which we would have been naturally led, if Adam had stayed sinless. For although no one in our fallen human race will recognise God as Father or the Author of salvation or favourable in any way until Christ steps in to make our peace, nevertheless it is one thing to grasp that God our Maker supports us by his power, rules us by his good Providence and showers us with every kind of blessing; it is another to lay hold of the gift of reconciliation offered to us in Christ. So, as the Lord is seen in the creation of the world and in the general teaching of Scripture, first simply as the Creator and only then as a redeemer in Christ, a dual knowledge of him appears. We will now look at these in order.

Although our minds cannot conceive of God without worshipping him, it is not enough to believe simply that he is the only being everyone ought to worship and adore, un-

less we are also convinced that he is the source of all goodness, and that we must seek for everything in him alone. I
am trying to say that we must be convinced not only that he
created the world, sustains it by his boundless power, governs it by his wisdom, keeps it going by his goodness, rules
the human race with justice, puts up with it in his love and
shields it with his protection, but also that there is not an
atom of light, wisdom or justice, power, integrity or truth to
be found anywhere but flowing from him and generated by
him. Obviously, then, we must learn to expect everything
from him and ask for it, gratefully acknowledging him as
the giver of all we receive. This awareness of divine perfection is the best way to learn piety from which true religion
springs. By 'piety' I mean the blend of reverence and love
to God which realising his blessings inspires. Until people
feel that they owe everything to God, that they are protected by his fatherly care and that he is the Author of all
their blessings, so that nothing should be sought apart from
him, they will never submit to him voluntarily. Indeed, unless they put their complete happiness in his hands, they
will never truly have their lives under his control.

2. Those who try to discover what the essence of God is,
only lead us astray with fruitless speculation. It is much
more in our interest to know what kind of being God is, and
what things are in line with his nature. What is the point of
believing with Epicurus in a god who takes no interest in the
world and loves to indulge himself? What is the point of
knowing a god to whom we cannot relate? The result of our
knowledge ought to be first, that we learn reverence and
awe and second, that we should be led under its guidance to
ask for every good thing from him, and when we receive it
to give thanks to him. How can the idea of God come to
mind without immediately making us think that since he
made us, we are bound by the law of creation itself to submit to his authority – that we owe our lives to him and that
we should refer everything we do to him? Otherwise it

surely follows that our lives are spoilt, if they are not planned in obedience to him, since our lives should be ruled by
his will. Our grasp of his nature is not clear unless we
acknowledge him to be the origin and fount of all goodness.
This would always lead to confidence in him and a longing
to stay close to him, if the depravity of man's mind did not
lead it away from the right approach. First of all, the 'pious'
mind does not create its own god, but looks only to the one
true God. Nor does it imagine any trait it likes for him, but
is happy to have him as the character which he reveals, always on guard against disobeying his Law and wandering
arrogantly from the right way. The man who knows God
like this, seeing how he is in control of everything, confides
in him as his guardian and protection and throws himself
completely on his faithfulness, realising that he is the
source of all blessing. If he has a problem or need, he immediately turns to God for protection and help; sure that he
is good and kind, he can rest confidently in him and does
not doubt that in his great goodness an answer will be found
for every need. He acknowledges God as Father and Lord,
and knows he must have respect for his authority, worship
his majesty in everything, try to further his glory and obey
his orders, reckoning him to be a fair Judge, having the
right to punish crimes severely, never forgetting the judgment seat. Rightly afraid of it, he controls himself, reluc-
tant to incur God's wrath. Nevertheless, he is not so terrified by the awareness of judgment that he tries to escape,
even if he could. Indeed he holds on to God as the avenger
of sin as much as the rewarder of good, because he realises
that both are part of his glory: he reserves punishment for
one and eternal life for the other. Anyway, it is not simply
fear of punishment that keeps him from sin. Even if there
was no hell, because he loves and reveres God as his Father
and honours and obeys him as his Master, he would spurn
the very idea of offending him. So this is pure and true religion: it is confidence in God coupled with genuine fear. This
fear comprises willing reverence and true worship as God

has commanded. All men give indiscriminate homage to God, but very few truly worship him. There are plenty of pretentious rituals but little sincerity of heart.

Chapter 3

The knowledge of God has been naturally implanted in the human mind.

1. It is beyond dispute that some awareness of God exists in the human mind by natural instinct, since God himself has given everyone some idea of him so that no one can plead ignorance. He frequently renews and sometimes increases this awareness so that all men, knowing that there is a God and that he is their maker, may be convicted in their own conscience when they do not worship him or give their lives to his service. If there should be an area where God was unknown, you would think it likely to be among the most primitive tribes, really remote from civilisation. But in fact there is evidence that there is no tribe so warlike, no race so uncivilised as to be without the conviction that there is a God. Even those which are very little different from animals seem to retain some religious awareness, because this universal conviction is firmly in the minds and hearts of all men. There has never been any part of the world, any city or any home without religion, proof that awareness of God is written on every heart. Even idol worship adds proof. We all know man's reluctance to admit anything superior to him, so when he chooses to worship objects of wood and stone rather than be thought to have no God, we can all see how indelible the impression of a God must be. It is more difficult to obliterate it from a man's mind than to crush natural emotions, as when, going against his natural pride, he spontaneously bows down before some lowly object to show reverence to God.

[2–3]

Chapter 4

The knowledge of God is suppressed or spoilt, inadvertently or deliberately.

1. Although experience shows that a seed of religion is put by God in everyone, barely one in a hundred really nurtures this seed, and there is no one in whom it grows to maturity, let alone yields fruit in season. While some men get caught up in superstitious practices and others deliberately revolt against God, the result is that all fail to know him fully and are so degenerate that true godliness cannot be found anywhere. As to the superstitious, I do not mean to imply that their great zeal frees them from guilt because their blindness is almost always linked with false pride and stubbornness. Vanity and pride are always present when men seek for God. Instead of rising above themselves as they ought to, they measure him by their own worldly folly and instead of solid investigation, they go away and humour their curiosity with useless guesswork. So they do not think of God in his true character, but imagine him to be like their own random ideas. Once this yawning chasm opens up, they cannot make a move without rushing headlong to destruction. With this idea of God, nothing they attempt to give him by way of worship or obedience is of any value in his sight, because it is not him they worship, but a transient figment of their own imagination. This false process is described aptly by Paul when he says that 'Although they claimed to be wise, they became fools' (Rom. 1:22). Earlier he said that 'they became vain in their imaginations', but so that no one should think them free of blame, he adds that they were deservedly blinded because, not content with serious enquiry and assuming for themselves more than they have any right to, they welcome darkness and delude themselves with stubborn and futile show. So

their stupidity, which is the result of vain curiosity, uncontrolled desire and excessive pride in the pursuit of forbidden knowledge, cannot be excused.

2. David's expression in Psalm 14:1, 'The fool says in his heart, "There is no God,"' is chiefly intended for those who suppress natural insight and deliberately make themselves foolish. We can see many people, after becoming hardened in a flagrantly sinful way of life, recklessly throw out all thoughts of God, even though they arise spontaneously in their hearts. To show how obnoxious this stupid action is, the Psalmist refers to them as those who deny that there is a God, because although they do not dispute his existence, they deny him his justice and Providence and represent him as sitting in heaven doing nothing. Nothing could be further from God's nature than to wash his hands of the government of the world, leaving it to chance and so condone men's crimes that they can do what they like unpunished. It follows that everyone who deludes himself that he is safe, when he has obliterated all fear of divine retribution, effectively denies the existence of God. After they have closed their eyes to the truth, and as a deserved punishment, God makes their hearts dull and unaware, so that seeing they cannot see. David is the best interpreter of his own words when he writes in Psalm 36:1 that the wicked has no 'fear of God before his eyes', and also says to himself, '"God has forgotten; he covers his face and never sees"' (Ps. 10:11). So although they are forced to acknowledge that there is a God, they take away his glory by denying his power. As Paul states, 'if we are faithless, he will remain faithful, for he cannot disown himself' (2 Tim. 2:13). So those who make for themselves a dead, dumb idol can truly be said to deny God. Also you can see that although they struggle with their convictions and try hard to banish God from their minds and from heaven too, their confused state is never sufficient to keep them from an occasional awareness of divine retribution. However, as no fear keeps them from

flying in the face of God, as long as they are carried along by their blind impulses, it has to be said that their attitude of mind to him is one of blatant disregard.

3. In this way, the futile excuses many people use to cover their superstitions are demolished. They think it enough to have some sort of religious fervour, however ridiculous, not realising that true religion must be according to God's will as the perfect measure; that he can never deny himself and is no mere spirit form to be changed around according to individual preference. It is easy to see how superstition with its false ideas makes a mockery of God while attempting to please him. It usually latches on to things which he regards as worthless and scorns or rejects things which he commands or in which we know he takes pleasure. So those who set up false worship merely exalt their own way-out ideas; indeed they would never dare to trifle with God like this, if they had not already shaped him according to their own childish designs. This vague and vacillating idea of God is said by Paul to be ignorance of God. 'Formerly, when you did not know God, you were slaves to those who by nature are not gods' (Gal. 4:8). And he states elsewhere that the Ephesians were 'without God' (Eph. 2:12) when they wandered about without any true knowledge of him. It does not make much difference, at least in this matter, whether you believe in the existence of one God or many, since in both cases, by departing from the one true God, you have nothing left but an obnoxious idol. We can only conclude with Lactantius that 'no religion is genuine that is not in accordance with truth.'

4. To this fault such people add another, that when they do think of God, it is against their will. They never approach him without being dragged into his presence and when there, instead of spontaneous worship springing from reverence for divine majesty, they feel only the compulsive

and cowering fear which divine judgment demands. They cannot escape this judgment and so are forced to dread it and hate it too. Those whose inclinations oppose God's justice, fervently wish that his tribunal for the punishment of sin could be overthrown. In feeling like this, they are fighting God, because justice is one of his essential attributes. They can see that they are always within his power and that resistance and evasion are impossible. So they fear and tremble. To avoid the impression of despising God's omnipotence, they turn to some kind of religious observance, always corrupting themselves with every kind of vice and crime until they have broken all God's laws and flouted his holiness. Token fear does not prevent them from luxuriating in sin. They choose to indulge their physical desires rather than control them with the restraint of the Holy Spirit. Since this shadow of religion is bogus and useless, it is easy to infer how different it is from the piety which is instilled into the hearts of true believers and from which alone genuine religion springs. And yet hypocrites try, in various twisted ways, to make a show of being near God when they are in fact running away from him. For while the whole of life ought to be one uninterrupted journey of obedience, these people rebel defiantly in all they do, and try to placate God with a few paltry sacrifices. They ought to serve him with integrity of heart and holiness of life; instead they attempt to gain his favour by frivolous deceit and trivial methods. They feel free to indulge themselves shamefully, because they imagine that they can please God with some futile expiation. Briefly, while their confidence should have been fixed in him alone, they reject him and rely on themselves or something else. Finally they get so confused in a maze of error, that the darkness of ignorance obscures and eventually extinguishes the sparks which were designed to show them the glory of God. However, the conviction that there is a God remains, like a plant which cannot be eradicated, though it is so rotten that it can only produce inferior fruit. We have even stronger evidence of the proposal I make (that a sense of God is naturally engraved in the human heart) in that even the ungodly are forced to acknowledge it. Such people joke about God at their leisure and talk insolently and garrulously, disparaging his power, but if despair overtakes them for any reason, it spurs them on to search for him. They make involuntary prayers, proving that they were not entirely unaware of him, but had deliberately suppressed feelings which ought to have been expressed long before.

Chapter 5

The knowledge of God is evident in his creation and continual rule of the world.

1. Since complete happiness is knowing God, in order that no one should be prevented from finding that happiness, he has kindly put in our minds the seed of true religion we have already spoken of and has also displayed his perfection in the whole structure of the universe. So he is constantly in our view and we cannot open our eyes without being made to see him. His nature is incomprehensible, far beyond all human thought, but his glory is etched on his creation so brightly, clearly and gloriously, that no one however obtuse and illiterate can plead ignorance as an excuse. So with absolute truth the Psalmist exclaims, 'He wraps himself in light as with a garment' (Ps. 104:2). It is as though he was saying that when God created the world for the first time, he put on outer clothes. He hung up gorgeous banners on which we see his perfection clearly portrayed. In the same place the Psalmist aptly compares the spread of the heavens with God's royal tent and says he 'lays the beams of his upper chambers on their waters. He makes the clouds his chariot and rides on the wings of the wind' (Ps. 104:3): sending out the wind and lightning as his swift messengers. Because the glory of his power and wisdom is more ablaze

in the heavens, it is frequently called his palace. Wherever you look, there is no part of the world however small that does not show at least some glimmer of beauty; it is impossible to gaze at the vast expanses of the universe without being overwhelmed by such tremendous beauty. So the author of the epistle to the Hebrews sensitively describes the visible world as an image of the invisible (Heb. 11:3). The superb structure of the world acts as a sort of mirror in which we may see God, who would otherwise be invisible. For the same reason, the Psalmist attributes language to heavenly bodies, a language which all nations can understand (Ps. 19:1). Evidence of God is far too obvious to escape the notice of anyone, however dull. The apostle Paul, stating this still more clearly, says ' ... since what may be known about God is plain to them, because God has made it plain to them. For since the creation of the world God's invisible qualities — his eternal power and divine nature — have been clearly seen, being understood from what has been made' (Rom. 1:19–20).
[2–10]

11. However, although the display which God gives of himself and his eternal kingdom is brightly reflected in the mirror of creation, we are so stupid and dim that we deserve no benefit from them. How few of us, as we look up to the skies or around at the earth, ever think of the Creator! We tend to overlook him and content ourselves with simply looking at the creation. In the matter of the supernatural, though things happen every day, very few acknowledge them as God's overruling providence. Most think of them as coincidence, produced by blind chance. Even when things hit us and we are forced to think of God and so form some impression of him, we immediately resort to worldly ideas and unworthy thoughts. So in our stupidity we tarnish divine truth. We differ from one another slightly in that we all adopt some individual error, but we are all the same in that we substitute blatant falsehood for the one living and true

God. This disease is not limited to dull, common intellects, but affects the finest, and those who, in other ways, are remarkably intelligent ...
[12–13]

14. Creation lights up all these bright lamps to demonstrate the glory of the Creator to us, all in vain. Although they shine on us from every direction, they are quite insufficient in themselves to lead us into the right way. They do, undoubtedly, throw out some sparks, but these are put out before they can give a brighter glow. So the apostle in the same place that he refers to the worlds as images of invisible things, adds that it is by faith we understand that they were framed by the Word of God (Heb. 11:3). He indicates that the invisible Godhead is indeed shown in creation, but that we have no eyes to see until they are enlightened through faith by inner revelation from God. When Paul says that what we can know of God is shown in the world he made, he does not mean the sort of display which can be grasped by man's intellect. On the contrary, he emphasises that this gives us no excuse (Rom. 1:19–20). And although he says elsewhere that we do not have to go far to search for God, because he lives within us (Acts 17:27), he shows in another passage to what extent this closeness to God serves any purpose. "'In the past, he let all nations go their own way. Yet he has not left himself without testimony: he has shown kindness by giving you rain from heaven and crops in their seasons; he provides you with plenty of food and fills your hearts with joy'" (Acts 14:16–17). Though God is not left without witnesses, and though he seeks to win men to knowledge of himself by countless acts of love, yet they insist on going their own way, making terrible mistakes.

15. Though we are lacking in natural ability which might enable us to rise to a pure, clear knowledge of God, the heaviness of heart which hinders us gives no room for excuse. We cannot plead ignorance, without being condemned by

our own consciences of laziness and ingratitude. It would be an odd excuse for man to pretend he has no ears to hear the truth, when dumb animals have voices to declare it; to state that he is unable to see what creatures without eyes can sense; to excuse himself on grounds of intellectual inability, when even creatures without reason can teach. So when we wander and go off track, we are rightly cut off from any sort of excuse, because everything indicates the right path. But while man is guilty of spoiling the seed of divine knowledge, so wonderfully placed in his mind, and preventing it from bearing genuine fruit, it is still true that we cannot get sufficient information from the simple testimony which the creatures give to the glory of their Creator. For no sooner do we gain some slight knowledge of God from looking at the world, than we turn from the true God and set up in his place an imaginary vision from our own brain. We draw the worship of justice, wisdom and goodness away from the fountain-head, transferring it elsewhere. Even more, by the wrong assessments we make, we either obscure or pervert God's creation so that we rob it of its glory and withhold the praise due to him.

Part II

GOD'S WORD AND GOD'S SPIRIT

Chapter 6

We need Scripture, as a guide and teacher, in coming to God as Creator.

1. So, since the radiance which meets our vision, both in the heavens and on earth, makes man's ingratitude unforgivable, and because God has given us all the same opportunity of seeing his deity reflected in creation in order to bring the whole human race under the same condemnation, something different and better is needed to lead us to our Creator God. To this end he has added the light of his Word to make himself known in salvation, giving that privilege to the ones he sees fit to bring into closer and more intimate relationship with himself. When he saw the vacillation of men's minds with no secure anchorage, he chose the Jews as his special people, and then hedged them in so that they would not go off course like others. In the same way, he successfully keeps us knowing him; otherwise, even those who seem strong by comparison with others would quickly fall away. As the elderly, or those with poor sight, can hardly make out the words in a book, but with the help of glasses can read clearly, so Scripture crystallises ideas about God which had been very confused, scatters the darkness and shows us the true God clearly. God has made a priceless gift in opening his own sacred mouth to instruct the Church, not leaving it to silent teachers alone. He not only proclaims that some sort of God must be worshipped, but simultaneously declares that he is the only God deserving reverence. He not only teaches his elect to be in awe of God, but sets himself forth as the God to whom they should direct their homage ...

2. ... So while men should consider the works of God seriously, since they have been put in this beautiful world for that purpose, they have a special responsibility to listen to his Word and benefit from it. It is not surprising that those who are born in darkness become increasingly obtuse, because the vast majority revel in their own proud ways, instead of being controlled by humble deference to the Word. If true religion is to shine on us we must grasp the necessity of beginning with teaching from above and that it is impossible for anyone to gain an atom of sound doctrine without being a disciple of Scripture. We take the first step towards true knowledge when we reverently take hold of the testimony God has graciously given about himself. Not only does a true and complete faith originate in obedience, but all sound knowledge does the same. In this matter God has, with amazing Providence, met man's need for all time.

3. If we think how ready the human mind is to forget God, how quick to follow every kind of error, how determined to create new and false religions, it will be easy to understand how it was essential to create a store of sound teaching which would be safe from loss by neglect, fading out in falsehood or being tainted by men's proud arrogance. It is clear that God anticipated that the impression of him given in earthly beauty would not be enough, and so gave the assistance of his Word to all whom he has graciously taught effectually. We too must follow this straight path if we sincerely long for true awareness of God. We must look in God's Word where his character is described accurately and vividly. It is depicted in his actions which are there assessed by the standard of eternal truth and not from our fallen standpoint. If we turn away from this, however fast we move, we shall never reach our goal because we are off course. We must realise that the glory of God's face, which even an apostle declares to be inaccessible (1 Tim. 6:16), is a sort of maze from which we cannot extricate ourselves

without the Word to act as a golden thread of guidance. It is better to limp along the right way than to run with great speed out of it. So the Psalmist repeatedly states (Pss. 93, 96, 97, 99 etc.) that superstition should be thrown out of the world so that pure religion can flourish. He then introduces God as reigning, referring not to the power which he possesses and employs in ruling the universe, but to the doctrine by which he maintains his rightful Lordship, because error can never be rooted out of the heart of man until true knowledge of God has been planted there.
[4]

Chapter 7

The witness of the Spirit is necessary to make certain the authority of Scripture. (The wicked falsehood of making its credibility depend on the judgment of the Church.)

1. Before going any further, it seems right to make some observations on the authority of Scripture, so that our minds may not only be ready to receive it thoughtfully, but have all doubts removed. When God's Word is acknowledged to be so, no one would be so brazen, unless he was stupid or insensitive, as to belittle the author. But, because we do not hear constant voices from heaven and the Scriptures are the only place in which God has chosen to record his truth for a perpetual reminder, the full authority in which the believer ought to hold them is not recognised unless they are thought to have come from heaven as distinctly as though God had spoken them. This subject should really be treated at great length, and considered in greater detail. My readers will excuse me for thinking more about what my scheme allows, than of the length this topic deserves ...
[2–3]

4. It is essential to pay attention to the point I have already made, that we cannot rely on the doctrine of Scripture until we are absolutely convinced that God is its Author. Its best authentication is the character of the one whose Word it is. The prophets and apostles do not boast of their own cleverness or any gifts as public speakers, nor do they lay stress on arguments. They appeal to the sacred name of God, so that the whole world may be brought into submission. Then it seems not merely probable but certain that God's name is not lightly nor falsely assumed. So if we want to find the best answer for our consciences and prevent them from being tossed around in a whirlpool of uncertainty, from wavering and stumbling at the slightest obstacle, our conviction of the truth of Scripture must be derived from a higher source than human guesswork, opinions and arguments, namely the hidden witness of the Spirit. True, if we choose to go the way of argument, it is easy to make a case, using all sorts of evidence, that if there is a God in heaven, the Law and the Prophecies and the Gospel must have come from him. Indeed even if the wisest and cleverest of men should oppose this view, and demonstrate all their powers of genius in the discussion, unless they are brazenly arrogant, they will be forced to agree that the Scripture shows clear proof of being spoken by God, and consequently of containing his divine truth. We shall see later how the volume of sacred Scripture far surpasses all other writings. More, if we study it with clear eyes and unbiased judgment, it will immediately display such divine authority as will quell our impertinent attacks and compel us to pay homage. However it is preposterous to attempt by discussion to bring about full faith in Scripture. True, if I had to oppose the cleverest enemies of God, I believe it would not be difficult to silence their blusterings, even though I am not specially able or eloquent. Without much difficulty I could squash the boastful ideas they mutter about in corners, if anything was to be gained by answering their petty objections. But although we may defend God's holy Word

against all opponents, it does not follow that we can establish in their hearts the conviction which faith demands. Unbelievers think that religion is a matter of opinion and so demand rational proof that Moses and the prophets were divinely inspired, if they are to have sufficient ground for belief. My reply is that the testimony of the Spirit is superior to reason. As God alone can truly bear witness to his own words, so these words will not be given complete acknowledgment in the hearts of men, until they are sealed by the inner witness of the Spirit. So the same Spirit, who spoke by the mouth of the prophets, must pervade our hearts, in order to convince us that they faithfully passed on the message entrusted to them by God. This link is best expressed by Isaiah in this way: "'My Spirit, who is on you, and my words that I have put in your mouth will not depart from your mouth, or from the mouths of your children, or from the mouths of their descendants from this time on and for ever'" (Isa. 59:21). Some sincere people feel distressed, because they cannot find clear proof ready to hand to silence the infidels who oppose the Word of God with impunity. They forget that the Spirit is called a pledge and seal to confirm the faith of the godly because until he enlightens their minds, they are tossed about on a sea of doubts.

5. We have established that those who are inwardly taught by the Holy Spirit accept Scripture implicitly, that Scripture, taking its own evidence along with it, does not stoop to be assessed by evidence and argument, but owes the absolute conviction with which we ought to receive it, to the testimony of the Spirit. Enlightened by him we no longer have to rest on our own judgment or that of others, that the Scriptures are from God. Rather we can feel completely sure, in a way far above human opinion and just as though we could see God's picture stamped on them, that they came to us from the very mouth of God, using men as his instruments. We do not ask for proof or evidence on which to rest our judgment, but we submit our intellect and opinion

to it as being immeasurably superior. We do not do this like those who tend to latch on to something unfamiliar and reject it when grasped, but because we are completely convinced that, in holding Scripture, we hold unassailable truth. We are not like unhappy creatures whose minds are enslaved by superstition, but we feel a divine energy living and breathing in it which encourages and inspires us to obey it willingly and with understanding, but with more life and power than could be exerted by human will and wisdom. So God rightly exclaims through Isaiah: "'You are my witnesses," declares the Lord, "and my servant whom I have chosen, so that you may know and believe me and understand that I am he'"(Isa. 43:10). This, then, is a conviction which does not ask for reasons, a knowledge which agrees with the most superior learning and in which the mind can rest more firmly and securely than in any arguments. In short it is a conviction which divine revelation alone can produce. I am stating no more than is the experience of every believer, though my words fall far short of reality. I will not linger on this subject because we will return to it. Can we simply grasp that the only true faith is that which God's Spirit seals on our hearts? The humble and receptive reader will be convinced by the promises contained in Isaiah that all the children of the renewed Church 'will be taught by the Lord' (Isa. 54:13). God bestows this priceless privilege only on his elect, whom he sets apart from the rest of mankind. The beginning of true doctrine is swift eagerness to hear the word of God. And God, by the mouth of Moses, demands to be heard like this: 'It is not up in heaven, so that you have to ask, "Who will ascend into heaven to get it and proclaim it to us so that we may obey it?" ... No, the word is very near you; it is in your mouth and in your heart' (Deut. 30:12, 14). Since God has chosen to reserve the treasure of true wisdom for his children, it is not surprising that there is so much ignorance and stupidity in the majority of men. In this majority, I include even those specially chosen, until they are grafted into the body of the Church. Isaiah indeed, while reminding us that the prophetical doctrine would prove hard to believe for unbelievers and also for Jews, who liked to be thought of as the household of God, adds the reason when he asks ' ... To whom has the arm of the Lord been revealed?' (Isa. 53:1) If, at any time, we are troubled at the small number of those who believe, let us remember that no one can understand the mysteries of God except those to whom it is given.

[Chapter 8]

Chapter 9

All the principles of godliness are undermined by fanatics who substitute revelations for Scripture.

1. ... The work of the Spirit promised to us is not to create new and unfamiliar revelations, or to coin some novel type of teaching by which we may be led away from the received doctrine of the Gospel, but to seal on our minds the very doctrine which the Gospel recommends.

2. So it is easy to understand that we must give careful attention both to the reading and hearing of Scripture if we want to get any benefit from the Spirit of God (just as Peter praises those who study prophetic teaching in depth (2 Pet. 1:19) although the light of the Gospel could be thought to take its place). Any spirit which bypasses the truth of God's Word, and suggests any other doctrine, is rightly suspected of pride and deceit. Since Satan transforms himself into an angel of light, what authority can the Spirit have over us unless he can be recognised by the same infallible sign? In fact he is singled out by the Lord with great clarity, but those wretched people go astray as if determined to destroy themselves by seeking the Spirit from themselves rather than from him. They say that it is an insult to subject the Spirit to Scripture, when everything is subject to him; as if

it could be dishonouring the Spirit to be always the same and in every way consistent with himself! True, if he was subjected to some other standard it might humiliate or restrict him, but as long as he is compared with himself how can he be harmed? I admit that he is brought to a test, but it is the one he has chosen to establish his majesty. Hearing his voice ought to be enough for us but in case Satan should creep in using his name, he wants us to recognise him by the image stamped on Scripture. The author of the Scriptures cannot change, or alter his appearance. As he was seen in the beginning, so he will be for ever. There is nothing dishonouring to him in this, unless we imagine it would be right for him to weaken and revolt against himself.

3. ... This is in no way inconsistent with what we said before, that we cannot be sure of the Word unless it is confirmed by the witness of the Spirit. The Lord has intertwined the truth of his Word and his Spirit in such a way that we respect the Word when the Spirit illumines it, enabling us to see God's face, and we welcome the Spirit, with no risk of error, when we recognise him in his Word. These are the facts. God did not put his Word in front of men to make a sudden splash, intending to get rid of it the moment the Spirit arrived. He employed the same Spirit, by whom he had given the Word, to complete his work by effectively confirming the Word. This was how Christ explained to the two disciples (Luke 24:27) that they must not ignore Scripture and look to their own wisdom, but must understand the Scriptures. In the same way, when Paul says to the Thessalonians 'Do not put out the Spirit's fire', he does not carry them away with empty speculation, divorced from the Word, but immediately adds, 'do not treat prophecies with contempt' (1 Thess. 5:19–20). By this he is obviously indicating that the light of the Spirit is quenched as soon as the prophetic word is scorned. What would these excitable enthusiasts say to that, who maintain that true enlightenment comes from dismissing God's

Word and latching on to any fantasy which springs to mind? God's children need to be very serious about this. Just as they feel that without God's Spirit they have no true light, so they know that the Word is the means by which the light of the Spirit comes. They recognise no other Spirit than the one who lived and spoke in the apostles – the Spirit by whose authority they are invited to listen to the Word every day.

[Chapters 10–12]

Part III

GOD THE TRINITY AND HIS CREATION

Scripture teaches from the beginning that God's one essence contains three persons.

[1–6]

7. Before going any further, it is necessary to prove the divinity of the Son and the Holy Spirit. Then we shall see how they differ from each other. When God's Word is given us in the Scriptures, it would be wrong to think of it as a fading voice, sent out on the air from somewhere beyond God, as in the messages given to patriarchs, and all the prophecies. The Word refers to God's eternal wisdom, by which all pronouncements and prophecies were inspired. As Peter proclaims (1 Pet. 1:11) the prophets of old spoke by the Spirit of Christ just like the apostles, and all who followed them as ministers of the Gospel. But as Christ had not yet appeared, obviously we understand that the Word was born of the Father before time began. If the Spirit for whom the prophets were channels, belonged to the Word, we cannot deny the inference that the Word was God himself. This is clearly demonstrated by Moses in his account of the creation, where he describes the Word as a link. Why does he specifically mention that God, in creating each of his works, said, Let there be this – let there be that, unless he wanted the unsearchable glory of God to shine in his image? I know the tub-thumpers could easily get round this, by saying that Word is used for order or command; but the apostles give the meaning much more accurately when they describe the worlds as created by the Son, who sustains everything by his powerful Word (Heb. 1:2). We can see here that Word is

used for the Son's command, and he himself is the very Word of the Father. No sane man could have any doubt as to Solomon's meaning, when he portrays wisdom as originating in God, presiding over the creating of the world and every divine work. It would be irrational to think there could be any temporary order at the time God chose to carry out his changeless and eternal will. And there was something even more amazing. Our Saviour said, 'My Father is always at his work to this very day, and I, too, am working' (John 5:17). In proclaiming by these words that he had always worked with the Father from the foundations of the world, he gives a clearer explanation of what Moses barely mentioned. The meaning is this: that God spoke in such a way that the Word had his own distinctive part in the work, so making it a shared operation. However, the clearest explanation is given by John when he states that the Word which was from the beginning, truly God and with God, was, together with the Father, the Maker of all things (John 1:3). He gives to the Word a substantial and permanent being, along with a definite individuality, clearly sharing how God spoke the world into existence. So, as all revelations from heaven are rightly described as the Word of God, so the highest place must be given to that specific Word, the source of all inspiration. As it is impossible for this Word to alter, it remains eternally one and the same as God. This Word is God.
[8–15]

16. As God has shown himself more clearly in the coming of Christ, so he has made himself more widely understood as three persons. Of the many proofs, let this one be enough. Paul connects God, faith and baptism and reasons from one to another (Eph. 4:5). So because there is one faith, he infers that there is one God; and because there is one baptism, he infers that there is one faith. Therefore, if by baptism we are initiated into the faith and worship of one God, we must, of course, believe that the one into whose name

we are baptised is the true God. And there can be no doubt that our Saviour wanted to proclaim, in a most positive statement, that the full light of faith can be seen, when he said 'Therefore go and make disciples of all nations, baptising them in the name of the Father and of the Son and of the Holy Spirit' (Matt. 28:19).

Since this is the same as being baptised into the name of the one God, who has been shown forth in the Father, the Son and the Holy Spirit, so it is obvious that the three persons, by whom God is known, coexist in the divine nature. Because faith ought not to be dashing around in all directions but should hold fast to God alone, it is obvious that if there were varieties of faith, there would have to be a variety of gods. So, because baptism is a sacrament, its unity assures us of God's unity. Moreover, it is self-evident that we must only be baptised into one God, because we make profession of faith in him in whose name we are baptised. So what does our Saviour mean, when he commands that baptism should be administered in the name of the Father, and the Son, and the Holy Spirit, if it is not that we are to be united in one faith in them? This is the same as stating that the Trinity is one God. So since we must believe that there is one God, and not more than one, we conclude that the Word and Spirit are of the very essence of God...

17. We also have to realise, though, that the Scriptures indicate a distinction between the Father and the Word, the Word and the Spirit; the greatness of the mystery reminds us of the reverence and seriousness we must have when discussing it. It seems to me that the words of Gregory Nazianzen cannot be bettered: 'I cannot think of the unity without being irradiated by the Trinity: I cannot distinguish between the Trinity without being carried up to the unity'. So let us be careful not to imagine a Trinity which will distract our minds, instead of concentrating on the unity. The words Father, Son and Holy Spirit definitely indicate a real distinction. We cannot think that they are simply titles

given to God to label his various functions. They indicate distinction but not division. The passages already quoted show that the Son has a life distinct from the Father. How could he be 'with' God unless he were distinct from the Father? Nor but for this could he have had his glory with the Father. In the same way, Christ distinguishes the Father from himself, when he says that there is another who bears witness of him (John 5:32; 8:16). There are words to the same effect in other places, that the Father made all things by the Word. This would be impossible if he was not in some way distinct from him. Besides, it was not the Father who came down to earth, but the one who came from the Father. Nor was it the Father who died and rose again, but the one whom the Father had sent. This distinction did not begin at the incarnation: it is clear that the only begotten Son had existed previously in the bosom of the Father (John 1:18). Who would dare to say that the Son entered his Father's bosom for the first time, when he came down from heaven to take on human nature? So he must have been there before and had his glory with the Father. Christ implies the distinction between the Holy Spirit and the Father, when he says that the Spirit proceeds from the Father, and between the Holy Spirit and himself, when he speaks of him as 'another', as he does when he promises that he will send another Counsellor and in many other instances (John 14:6; 15:26; 14:16).

18. I am not sure whether it is helpful to use parallels from human affairs to illustrate this distinction. The Church fathers sometimes do so, but at the same time they admit that there is disparity in any comparison. So I am very wary of presumption in this, in case some thoughtless word may give the malicious person an opportunity for slander, or the ignorant person may be led astray. It would be wrong, however, not to comment on a distinction which is referred to in Scripture. This is the distinction: the beginning of action is attributed to the Father, the fount and source of every-

thing; wisdom, knowledge and planning the action is the Son's province, while the energy and skill in action is assigned to the Spirit. Further, although the eternal nature of the Father also belongs to the Son and Spirit (since God could never be without his own wisdom and energy) and although there could be no place for first or last in eternity, the distinction of order is not meaningless or unnecessary. The Father is thought of first, then the Son from him, and finally the Spirit from both. Everyone thinks naturally of God first, then the wisdom which springs from him and finally the energy by which he carries out his plans. Because of this, the Son is said to be from the Father alone, but the Spirit from both Father and Son. References come in many places but in none so clearly as in the eighth chapter of Romans, where the same Spirit is called, indiscriminately, the Spirit of Christ and the Spirit of him who raised up Christ from the dead. Quite right. Peter also testifies (2 Pet. 1:21) that it was the Spirit of Christ which inspired the prophets, though the Scriptures so often say that it was the Spirit of God the Father.

19. This distinctiveness in no way interferes with God's perfect unity, because the Son can be proved to be one with the Father (for he constitutes one Spirit with him) and the Spirit to be no different from the Father and Son (for he is the Spirit of the Father and the Son). God's whole nature is seen in each of the persons; their only difference is that each has his own individual existence. The whole Father is in the Son and the whole Son in the Father, as the Son himself declares, 'I am in the Father, and ... the Father is in me' (John 14:10).

No ecclesiastical writer would allow that the one is separated from the other by any difference of being. 'The names we use to distinguish between the different persons of Trinity,' says Augustine, 'refer to the relationships of the persons to each other, not to their common substance or nature – which is one.' In this way, the ideas of the Church fathers, which might seem to conflict, are to be reconciled. At one time they teach that the Father is the origin of the Son; at another they maintain that the Son has divinity and essential being from himself, and therefore has the same origin as the Father. Augustine explains this discrepancy clearly and well when he says 'Christ, as to himself, is called God; as to the Father he is called Son'. And again: 'The Father, as to himself, is called God; as to the Son he is called Father. He who, as to the Son, is called Father, is not Son; and he who, as to himself, is called Father and he who, as to himself, is called Son, is the same God.' So when we speak of the Son alone, without reference to the Father, we correctly state that he exists without a cause, and so call him the only beginning; but when we want to convey the relationship he bears to the Father, we rightly make the Father the beginning of the Son ...

20. Let all who are really serious and happy in the faith accept this helpful idea: When we profess to believe in one God, the name 'God' represents his essential being which is made up of three persons or individuals. So whenever the name of God is used in a general sense, the Son and the Spirit are implied just as much as the Father. But when the Son is linked with the Father, a relationship comes into play, and so we must distinguish between two persons. Then as the individual beings are ranked in order, the principle and origin are in the Father and whenever Father and Son, or Father and Spirit, are mentioned together, the name of God refers specially to the Father. In this way the unity of being is kept, while attention is given to order. However it in no way detracts from the divinity of Son and Spirit. Just as the apostles declared the Son of God to be the one whom Moses and the prophets called Jehovah, we too must always assume a unity of being. We believe that to call the Son a different God from the Father is a hateful blasphemy, because the simple name 'God' does not allow for anything akin to it, nor can God, considered in himself, be

described as this or that. The name Jehovah, taken generally, may be applied to Christ. This is clear from Paul's
words, 'Three times I pleaded with the Lord to take it away
from me.' After giving the reply, 'My grace is sufficient for
you,' he adds, 'that Christ's power may rest on me' (2 Cor.
12:8, 9). It is obvious that the name of the Lord is used for
Jehovah, and so to restrict it to the person of the Mediator
would be puerile and shallow, since Paul's purpose here is
not to compare Father and Son. Also we know that the
apostles consistently used the word 'Lord' in place of
'Jehovah', in keeping with the accepted Greek usage. For
instance, Paul called on the Lord in the same sense in which
Peter quotes Joel, 'And everyone who calls on the name of
the Lord will be saved' (Acts 2:21; Joel 2:32). Where this
name is specifically applied to the Son, there is a different
reason for it, as the context will show. It is enough for now
to remember that Paul, after praying simply to God, immediately adds the name of Christ. So also the Spirit is
called simply 'God' by Christ himself. There is nothing to
stop us thinking that the entire Godhead is spiritual, and in
it are included Father, Son and Spirit. This is plain from
Scripture. Just as God is referred to as Spirit, so the Holy
Spirit also, in that he has existence within the whole being,
is said to be both of God and from God.
[21–29]

Chapter 14

**Scripture shows that even in the creation of the
universe, the true God is distinguished from false
gods by certain marks.**

[1–19]

20. Since we are placed in such a beautiful world, we should
take a reverent delight in God's work of creation. As we

have stated elsewhere, it is the first sign of faith (though not the greatest) to realise that everything we look at is made by God, and to think reverently about his purposes in creation. So that we can grasp all this aright, it is vital to study the history of creation as given by Moses. From this we learn that God created the heavens and earth out of nothing by the power of his Word and his Spirit. After this he made all sorts of animate and inanimate things, arranging them in perfect order and giving to each its particular nature, work and position. As everything was liable to corruption, he provided for the perpetuation of each species, in ways appropriate to each. When heaven and earth had been richly adorned and generously supplied with everything like a great mansion, exquisitely designed and furnished, finally man was created. Because of his grace and gifts, he was the most splendid specimen of all God's works. Now, as I have no intention of giving the creation story in detail, I will remind my reader again that the best course is to learn all about it from Moses and others who have given such a careful and true account.

21. I will not dwell at length on our aim in considering God's works. This has been explained elsewhere and a few words will be enough now. Of course if we were to try and match God's amazing wisdom, power, justice and goodness in forming the world, by the splendour of our diction, nothing could be good enough. But we can be quite sure that the Lord wants us to think in this way, so that as we look at the riches of his wisdom and goodness shown in creation as in a mirror, we may not just give them a passing glance, but gaze on them at length. However, as this is an instruction manual, I cannot get involved in things which deserve lengthy discussion. So, to be concise, let the reader be sure he has a genuine understanding of the character of God as the Creator of the world, first by never forgetting the glorious perfection God shows in his creatures and second by applying what he sees to himself, keeping it deep in his

heart. We carry out the first duty when we consider how great the Architect must be who designed the starry myriad so amazingly that it would be impossible to imagine a more superb sight. He made some fixed stars; others are freer but still have limits and everything is balanced to mark out day and night, months, years and seasons. We also do well to notice his power in sustaining such a vast universe, guiding the swift revolutions of heavenly bodies and so on. These few examples are enough to explain what is meant by recognising divine perfection in creation.

22. Now we must look at the other method, which has a closer relevance to faith. That is, when we see how God has destined everything for our good and our salvation, we also realise his power and grace in our hearts and in the great blessings he has given. This moves us to have confidence in him and to pray, praise and love. Also, as I said before, the Lord himself, by his design in creation, has shown that he made everything for man's good. It is important to notice that he divided the creation of the world into six days, although he could have done it all in a second. So he was glad to show his fatherly provision and care for us, in that before he made man, he prepared what he could see would be useful and good for him. How ungrateful it is then to doubt the love of this most perfect Parent, when we see how he cared for us even before we were born! It is so wrong to waver in distrust that we might one day be deserted in our need by such kindness! Again, Moses tells us that everything in the world is freely placed at our disposal (Gen. 1:28; 9:2). Nothing to do with our safety will ever be missing. In conclusion, whenever we call God the Creator of heaven and earth, let us remember that he can give us whatever he chooses and that we are his children, whom he has undertaken to care for and bring to himself. We can expect good things from him alone and have full assurance that he will never let us be without everything necessary for salvation, so that we have to turn elsewhere. We can turn to him in

prayer with all our longings and see his hand in every blessing. As we praise him, drawn by his great goodness and
generosity, we must apply ourselves wholeheartedly to love
and to serve him.

Chapter 15

**The state in which man was created. (The faculties
of the soul – the image of God – free will – the original righteousness of our nature.)**

1. We must now talk about the creation of man, not only because it is the noblest and most perfect example of his justice, wisdom and goodness but (as we said at the beginning)
also because we cannot clearly and rightly know God, unless we know ourselves. This knowledge is twofold: it re-
lates firstly, to the condition in which we were originally
created and secondly, to our condition immediately after
Adam's Fall. It wouldn't be much use to know how we were
created if we were unaware of the corruption and degrada-
tion of our nature as a result of the Fall. For the moment we
will restrict ourselves to thinking about our nature in its
original perfection. Indeed, before we descend to the
wretched condition into which man has fallen, it is vital to
see what he was at first. We need to be careful not to look
only at the natural ills of man and then appear to attribute
them to the Author of nature. The irreverent person defends himself by arguing that everything evil comes from
God and doesn't hesitate to blame him. Those who are
rather more reverent still make nature an excuse for their
sinfulness, not realising that they too are bringing a charge
against God, on whom the blame would fall if it could be
proved that evil was intrinsic to nature. So because the
natural man is always on the lookout for ruses by which he
thinks he can shift the blame for his own wickedness
elsewhere, we must strenuously guard against this vicious

habit. We have to assess the Fall of the human race in such a way that there can be no excuses and God's justice can be vindicated against all attack. We shall see later how far man has come from the purity originally given to Adam. When he was formed out of the dust of the ground, a restriction was placed on his pride. How stupid it would be for those who not only live in clay houses but are themselves made partly from dust and ashes, to glory in their brilliance! But Adam might well glory in the bounty of his Maker, who not only deigned to give life to a clay vessel but made it also the dwelling place of an immortal spirit.

2. Now there can be no question that man consists of body and soul. By soul we mean an immortal, though created, being, which is the nobler part. Sometimes it is called a spirit. When the two terms are used together, they have a different meaning, but when spirit is used by itself, it is the same as soul, as when Solomon, referring to death, says that the spirit returns to God who gave it (Eccles. 12:7). Christ also, in commending his spirit to the Father (Luke 23:46) and Stephen his to Christ (Acts 7:59), simply meant that when the soul is freed from the prison-house of the body, God becomes its eternal keeper. Those who imagine that the soul is called a spirit because it is a breath of energy infused into the body by God, but having no being of its own, make a grave error. Both human experience and the whole tenor of Scripture make this clear. It is certainly true that men, who cling to the things of this world, have little understanding. Worse, being alienated from the Father of light, they are so swamped in darkness as to think there is no life after death. However the light is not so completely extinguished that all sense of immortality is lost. Conscience, which can distinguish between good and evil, responds to the judgment of God and so is proof positive of an immortal spirit. How could movement devoid of being approach the judgment seat of God and then terrify itself with the thought of its guilt? The body cannot be touched by fear

of spiritual punishment. This can only affect the soul, which again proves its existence. Finally, the knowledge of God in itself proves that souls which soar beyond this world must be immortal: it would be impossible for some ephemeral energy to reach the very fountain of life ...
[3]

4. The concept of man in the image of God emerges clearly as we see the skills in which he excels, and which reflect God's glory. However, a more accurate assessment still comes from looking at God's remedy for sin. It is undeniable that when Adam fell from grace, he became alienated from God. So, although we know that the image of God was not completely wiped out, it was so damaged that what remains is an ugly deformity. Our salvation begins with that new start which we receive from Christ. This is why he is called the second Adam, because he restores us to wholeness. Although Paul, contrasting the quickening Spirit which believers receive from Christ with the living soul created in Adam (1 Cor. 15:45), commends the former, he does not deny that the purpose of regeneration is to renew us in God's image. In Colossians 3:10 he states that the new man is renewed in the image of the one who created him. Again we read 'put on the new self, created to be like God in true righteousness and holiness' (Eph. 4:24). Now we must look at the details Paul includes in the new life. First he mentions knowledge, then true righteousness and holiness. So we infer that in the beginning God's image was evident by clear intellect, upright heart and integrity in every part. This has to be a brief summary, but the principle remains that what is of primary importance in restoration must also have been pre-eminent in creation. Paul says that as we gaze on the glory of Christ with unveiled face, we are transformed into his image (2 Cor. 3:18). Christ, of course, is the most perfect image of God and as we are renewed in him, we can bear the same image in knowledge, purity, righteousness and true holiness. The idea that the image is

physical can be dismissed. The passage in 1 Corinthians 11:7, in which man alone is called the image and glory of God, obviously refers to civil order. The 'image' includes anything which has relevance to spiritual and eternal life. John says the same when he declares that the light which was from the beginning in the eternal Word of God, was the light of man (John 1:4). His aim is to praise God's grace in making man excel the other animals, but at the same time he shows how he was formed in God's image. He separates him from the common herd, because he has the light of intellect and not merely animal existence. The image of God shone in all its glory in Adam before the Fall, but then it was tainted and almost obliterated. Nothing was left but a ruin, confused, mutilated and blemished. God's image can again be partially seen in the elect, as they are born again by the Spirit, but its full glory will only be seen in heaven ... [5–6]

7. ... We can establish that the soul consists of two parts, the intellect and the will. The work of the intellect is to make distinction between good and bad, and the function of the will is to choose and follow what the intellect says is good, rejecting what is bad. The intellect is like a guide for the soul, and the will waits for its direction. Aristotle rightly taught that in the area of physical desire, choices made seem to be in line with intellectual judgment. Intellect governs the will ...

8. So God has given intellect to the soul of man, so that he may discern good from evil and have the light of reason. He has also given will, by which choices are made. At creation, man had these gifts to perfection, when reason, intelligence, wisdom and judgment not only ruled his earthly life but enabled him to reach up to God and eternal joy. Then choice was added to control the appetites, but the will was always under the authority of reason. In this moral state, man had free will by which he could choose eternal life. It

would not be right to introduce the matter of predestination here, because we are looking at man's nature. Adam could have remained upright if he had chosen; he fell of his own volition. It was because his will could have taken him in either direction and he had received no firmness of purpose, that he fell so easily. He had free choice of good and evil. In his mind there had been the utmost integrity and all the potential for obedience, but he ruined its virtue and destroyed himself.

Philosophers who looked for a complete building in a ruin and order in chaos, found themselves utterly confused. They started from the premiss that man could not have been a rational animal unless he had free choice of good and evil. They also imagined that the distinction between virtue and vice was destroyed if man did not live his life by his own decisions. This would all have been logical if there had been no change in man. Because these thinkers are unaware of such a change, it is not surprising that they are confused. But those who profess to be disciples of Christ and still maintain that man has free will, despite his being lost and overwhelmed in spiritual destruction, labour under a big delusion. They hold an indiscriminate mixture of inspired doctrine and philosophical opinion, and miss the truth in both. To sum up, we need to remember that man at his first creation was very different from all men since then. Because they descended from him after he was corrupted, they inherited his imperfection. At first, every part of the soul was created for uprightness. There was soundness of mind and freedom of will to choose the good. If anyone complains that it was vulnerable because its power was weak, I have to answer that the honour conferred was enough to take away all excuses. For surely God could not be restricted to making man so that he either could not or would not sin? Such a nature might have been superior, but to argue with God, as though he were compelled to give this nature to man, is the height of injustice. He had absolute right to decide how much or how little he would give. Why he did not strengthen man with the virtue of perseverance is hidden from us; the wisest course for us is soberly to keep within the limits of what has been revealed to us. Man had received the power, if he had the will, but he did not have the will which would have given the power! This would have resulted in perseverance. However after he had received so much, there is no excuse for wilfully bringing death upon himself. God was not bound to give him more than his intermediate and transient will, so that from man's Fall he might find material for his own glory.

Part IV

GOD'S PROVIDENCE

Chapter 16

God by his power supports and maintains the world which he created. He rules each and all of its parts by his Providence.

1. It would be cold and unfeeling to picture God as a temporary Creator, who completed his work and then left it. Here we differ from the unbeliever in asserting that God's power is obvious in the ongoing world situation as well as in creation. Although evil men are compelled to move towards the Creator, simply from observing the earth and sky, faith has its own way of giving total worship to God for his creation. The passage of the apostle we have already quoted underlines this fact, that by faith we understand that the worlds were framed by the Word of God (Heb. 11:3). Without reference to God's Providence we cannot understand the full force of what is meant by his being the Creator, however much we may seem to understand it with our minds and confess it with our mouths. The carnal mind, when it has glimpsed the power of God in creation, stops there. At most it considers only the wisdom, power and goodness evidenced by the Author of such work, or some general factor on which the power of motion depends and which keeps the world going. To sum up: it imagines that everything is maintained by the divine energy infused into them at the beginning. But faith must go far deeper. After realising that there is a Creator, it must then infer that he is also Governor and Preserver, not just because he can produce a kind of general motion in the machine of the universe, as well as in each of its parts, but because by his special Providence he sustains and cares for everything he has

made down to the smallest sparrow! So David, after briefly stating that the world was created by God, immediately refers to the ongoing work of Providence: 'By the word of the Lord were the heavens made, their starry host by the breath of his mouth.' 'From heaven the Lord looks down and sees all mankind' (Ps. 33:6, 13, etc.). He adds other observations to the same effect. Not everyone argues so cogently, but because it would not make sense to say that human affairs are managed by God unless he was the Maker of the world, and no one could seriously believe that he is its Creator without feeling convinced that he takes care of his works. David, with good reason and beautiful logic, leads us from the one to the other. On the whole, in fact, philosophers teach, and the human mind grasps, that everything in the world is empowered by the secret inspiration of God. However, they do not reach the height to which David rises, along with all true believers, when he says:

> These all look to you to give them their food at the proper time. When you give it to them they gather it up; when you open your hand, they are satisfied with good things. When you hide your face, they are terrified; when you take away their breath, they die and return to the dust. When you send your Spirit, they are created, and you renew the face of the earth (Ps. 104:27–30).

Indeed, though they agree with Paul that in God 'we live and move and have our being' (Acts 17:28), they are far from understanding fully the grace which he commends, because they have no interest in the special care which shows God's fatherly love.
[2]

3. God claims omnipotence for himself, and wants us to acknowledge it. God's omnipotence is not futile, idle and inactive as some theologians pretend, but caring, effective,

energetic and always active. It is not an omnipotence which can only serve as a general influence in uncertainty (like ordering a stream to stay inside a prescribed channel), but one which focuses on specific and definite events. God is accepted as omnipotent, not because he has power whether he acts or not, nor because by some general instinct he maintains the order of creation, but because, in controlling heaven and earth by his Providence, he so overrules everything that nothing happens without his approval. The verse in the Psalms which says 'he does whatever pleases him' (Ps. 115:3) refers to his sure and certain plan. It would not be enough to interpret the Psalmist's words philosophically, to mean that God is the primary agent because he is the origin and cause of all activity.

The believers' comfort in trouble is that everything they endure is ordained and commanded by God and that they are in his hands. If God's rule is over all his works, we would be foolish to restrict it to the natural order of things. Those who keep God's Providence within narrow limits, as if he let everything be carried along by some constant law of nature, not only deny him his glory but deprive themselves of a valuable doctrine. Nothing could be more pathetic than the thought of man at the mercy of unpredictable elements, and if it were true, God's particular goodness towards each individual would be seriously damaged. David comments (Ps. 8:2) that babies at their mothers' breasts celebrate God's glory, because, from the moment of birth, they find nourishment prepared for them by his loving care. Unless we are obtuse, we must be aware that some mothers have plenty of milk and others hardly any, in line with God's discretion to feed one child well and another not so well. Those who pay homage to God's omnipotence derive a double blessing. The one to whom heaven and earth belong is more than able to reward them, and they can rest secure in his protection. Everything that could harm them is under his control: even Satan, with all his malevolence, is on a tight rein and no danger can threaten the believer unless

God wills it. This is the only way in which wild and faithless fears, aroused by the dangers which surround us, can be quietened. And they are faithless fears when we tremble at any threat from created things, as if in themselves they had power to hurt us, or as if they could harm us randomly or by chance, at will, or as if God was not sufficient protection for us. So Jeremiah tells the children of God not to 'be terrified by signs in the sky, though the nations are terrified by them' (Jer. 10:2). He does not condemn every kind of fear. But as unbelievers shift control of the world from God to the stars, imagining that happiness or misery depends on their forecasts and not on divine will, their trust which ought to be in God alone is transferred to stars and comets. Those who are wary of such superstition should realise that no created thing can act randomly. Everything is controlled by God's secret purpose, and nothing can happen except by his knowledge and will.

4. By Providence we do not mean that God sits idly in heaven, looking on at events in the world, but that he is at the helm overruling everything. It extends to action as well as vision. When Abraham said to his son 'God himself will provide' (Gen. 22:8) he did not mean simply that God knew the future, but he was handing over the whole matter to the will of one whose business it is to bring difficult situations to a happy conclusion. So we see that Providence consists of action, not merely foreknowledge. Another mistake is to think God controls only in a muddled vague way, giving impetus to the universe but not specifically directing the movements of individuals. This is inexcusable. According to those who support this view, there is nothing in such universal Providence to prevent casual movement in creation or to prevent man from acting haphazardly, according to the free choice of his will. In this way they make man God's partner: God by his power gives man the ability to act in harmony with his nature, but man controls his own actions at will. Their doctrine is that the world, men's affairs and

they themselves are ruled by God's power but not his purpose. I will not talk of the Epicureans (what a wretched nuisance they have always been!), who dream of an inactive and lazy God, and others just as unsound, who have always misrepresented God as ruling the upper regions, leaving the lower to Fate. Even dumb animals protest at such folly!

Now I want to refute a very common opinion. This concedes to God certain random activity, but denies the most important thing: that he disposes and directs everything to the end he designs by his unsearchable wisdom. By withholding government of the world, it makes God ruler in name only and not in fact. What is meant by government, if it is not to preside in such a way that you rule the destiny of those under you? However, I do not completely deny a universal Providence, if it is allowed that the world is governed by God, not only in maintaining the order of nature but also in taking special charge of each individual. It is true, certainly, that all species are motivated by a secret natural instinct, as if they respond to God's command and spontaneously follow his appointed course. Here we may refer to our Saviour's words, that he and his Father have always been at work from the beginning (John 5:17); also the words of Paul that 'For in him we live and move and have our being' (Acts 17:28) and the words of the writer to the Hebrews, who when wanting to prove the divinity of Christ says that he upholds 'all things by his powerful word' (Heb. 1:3). Some people by emphasising general Providence obscure the special, which is so definitely and clearly taught in Scripture that it is puzzling anyone can doubt it. Indeed, some who adopt this falsehood are forced to modify their doctrine by adding that many things are done by God's special care. But they wrongly restrict this to specific acts. What we must prove is that single events are ordered by God and that every event comes from his intended will. Nothing happens by chance.

[5–7]

8. Those who want to discredit this doctrine disparage it by comparing it with the Stoic dogma of Fate. The same charge was brought against Augustine. We don't want to argue about words, but we do not allow the term 'Fate', both because it is among those that Paul teaches us to avoid as heathen innovations and also because the obnoxious term is an attempt to attach a stigma to God's truth. The dogma itself is wrongly and maliciously imputed to us. Unlike the Stoics we do not picture a Fate consisting of an endless chain of causes and a type of involved sequence within nature, but we believe that God is the disposer and ruler of everything. From furthest eternity, he ruled on what he should do, according to his own wisdom, and now, by his power, he carries out what he decided then. So we maintain that, by his Providence, not only heaven and earth and all inanimate things, but also the minds and wills of men are controlled in such a way that they move precisely in the course he has destined. You may well ask whether anything happens by chance or is unforeseen. Basil the Great spoke the truth when he said that 'fortune' and 'chance' are heathen terms, which can have no room in the believer's mind. If all success is a blessing from God, and tragedies are his curse, there is no place left in human affairs for fortune and chance. We ought to be influenced by Augustine's words: 'In my writings against the Academics,' he writes, 'I regret having used the term "fortune" so often; although I did not intend to imply a goddess by it, but chance happenings, whether good or evil.' ... Augustine consistently teaches that if anything is left to luck, the world moves at random. And although he states elsewhere, that everything is carried out partly by man's free will and partly by God's Providence, he also shows clearly enough his real meaning. This is that men are controlled by Providence, since it would be absurd to believe that anything happens without God's ordination, because then it would happen at random. For this reason, he also excludes any happening which depends on human will, stating in clear terms that no

cause must be looked for except the will of God. When he uses the term permission, he means that the will of God is the supreme and primary cause of everything, because nothing happens without his order or permission. He certainly does not picture God sitting idly in a watch-tower, allowing anything to happen. The will which he represents as intervening is active, and could not otherwise be regarded as a cause.

[9]

Chapter 17

How to use this doctrine for our benefit.

1. Such is the tendency of the human mind to indulge in hair-splitting, that it becomes almost impossible for those who do not discern the correct use of this doctrine to avoid bewildering problems. So it is right to refer now to the purpose of Scripture in teaching that everything is divinely ordained. First, the Providence of God must be thought of in relation to the past and the future. Second, in overruling everything, it works in a variety of ways. Last, God's plan is to show that he takes care of the whole human race, but is specially protective of the Church, which he blesses with a more intimate direction.

Although the fatherly approval and kindness of God (as well as his judgment) are obvious in the whole realm of Providence, occasionally the thought can rise that human affairs are whirled around by the blind impulse of fortune. Our carnal nature makes us speak of God as though he is amusing himself by tossing men around in a game. If only we could calm down and set ourselves to learn the true situation, we would see that God's plan is highly rational. His purpose is either to develop patience in his people, correct their vices, control their impurity, accustom them to self-denial and stir them from laziness; or it is to humble the proud, defeat the ungodly and frustrate their scheming.

There is so much that we are unaware of, but we can rest assured that everything is safe with him and so exclaim with David, 'Many, O Lord my God, are the wonders you have done. The things you planned for us no-one can recount to you; were I to speak and tell of them, they would be too many to declare' (Ps. 40:5). While adversity ought to remind us of our sins, so that the punishment may lead us to repentance, we see how Christ teaches that God, in his wisdom, plans to do more than punish everyone as he deserves. So he says of the man who was born blind, 'Neither this man nor his parents sinned, but this happened so that the work of God might be displayed in his life' (John 9:3). In this case, where tragedy seems to take place even before birth, our carnal minds protest, as if God is being harsh in making the innocent suffer. But Christ declares that, if only we had eyes to see, we would realise that the glory of his Father shines out in this situation. We must have humility, not compelling God to render an account, but so acknowledging his hidden purposes that we recognise his will must be best. When the sky is overcast and a violent storm breaks, the darkness and thunder terrify us and we think everything is in a state of confusion, when, in fact, everything goes on serenely up above. In the same way, when our lives are in turmoil so that we cannot think straight, we should still believe that God, in the pure light of his justice and wisdom, keeps our problems under his control, and finds the right solution. Many people are extremely foolish in this area; they dare to assess God's action from their own point of view, discuss his hidden motives and rashly pass instant judgment on things they cannot know about. What could be more absurd than to show restraint towards our equals, and suspend judgment rather than be called impetuous, while we arrogantly insult God's hidden wisdom when we ought to respect it.

[2]

3. ... The scoffers make such a commotion with their stupid arguments that almost everyone is confused. If, they say, the Lord has planned the moment of our death, it is inevitable and there is nothing we can do about it. So, when people try to avoid dangers on a journey, or call in the doctor to obtain drugs for the sake of health, or abstain from certain foods to protect a weak constitution, or refuse to live in a run-down house, the scoffers say they are trying to find ways of achieving their own ends. They maintain that these are vain attempts to alter God's will because his sure command fixes the limits of life and death, health and sickness, peace and war and everything else which men try to achieve or avoid by their own efforts. These shallow people imply that the prayers of the faithful must be misguided and unnecessary, because they beg the Lord to act in things which he has decreed from eternity. Attributing whatever happens to the Providence of God, they excuse the person who has deliberately planned it. Has a murderer killed an innocent man? He has only, they say, carried out God's will. Has someone committed theft or adultery? He is merely the one who carries out what the Lord has ordained. Has a son stood by, waiting for his parents to die, without trying to do anything? He must not oppose God, who had planned it all from eternity. In this way, all crimes are called virtues, because they must be according to God's will.

4. When it comes to future events, Solomon reconciles human deliberation with divine Providence quite easily. While he scorns the stupidity of those who dare to undertake anything without God's help, as if they were not under his control, he also states, 'In his heart a man plans his course, but the Lord determines his steps' (Prov. 16:9). This suggests that God's eternal decrees in no way prevent us from providing for ourselves, and arranging all our affairs (subject to his Lordship). The reason for this is clear. The one who has fixed the boundaries of our life, has also entrusted us with the care of it, given us the means to

safeguard it, warned us of the dangers which threaten us, and supplied remedies so that we may not be overwhelmed. Now, our duty is clear: since the Lord expects us to defend our lives, we must do so; since he offers his help, we must take it; since he warns us of danger, we must be careful; and since he supplies remedies we must use them. Some will say that if a danger is not fatal, it will not hurt us, and if it is fatal, nothing can be done. But what if these hazards are not fatal simply because the Lord has given you the means to fend them off and surmount them? Try to match your reasoning with the way God actually works: you infer that no precautions need be taken in danger, because if it is not fatal you will escape anyway; whereas the Lord urges you to take precautions, just because he does not will it to be fatal. These crazy protesters overlook what is staring them in the face: that the Lord has given men the ability to think and to be careful so that they may use it (in submission to his Providence) to preserve their lives. The opposite is true: by neglect and laziness, they bring upon themselves the troubles he has linked with such behaviour. How is it that a careful man, in taking safeguards, avoids impending danger, while a foolish man, through thoughtless daring, perishes? It must be that wisdom and folly are, in both instances, instruments of divine dispensation. God has chosen to conceal all future events from us, that we may prepare for them in uncertainty, and never cease to employ the remedies we have been given, until all hurdles have been overcome or have proved too much for us. So, as I said before, the Providence of God does not act in itself; but, by working in different ways, it assumes as it were a visible form.
[5–8]

9. Despite all this, the Christian should not ignore lesser causes. He should consider those who help him as ministers of divine goodness and not overlook them, as though their kindness deserved no thanks. He should feel under real ob-

ligation, admit to it and try all in his power to reciprocate.
In short, he will honour and praise God as the principal Author of all the blessings he receives, but will also respect the people who are God's agents. He will be aware that it is God's will that he should feel under obligation to those by whom God has chosen to show him kindness. If he suffers loss through carelessness or stupidity, he will believe it was the Lord's will it should be so, but at the same time he will lay the blame at his own door. If someone for whom he should have cared, but whom he has neglected, dies of a disease, he will not excuse himself, but will feel it was his fault. In the case of theft or murder, fraud and malice, he will be even less able to justify it on the grounds of divine Providence. Rather he will recognise clearly in each crime the distinction between the justice of God and the sin of man. In future events, he will notice lesser causes. If he receives help from other people, he will recognise it as God's blessing, but he will not therefore fail to take measures or be slow in accepting help. He will avail himself of every sort of assistance, see them as hands held out by the Lord and true instruments of divine Providence. As he cannot know the outcome of any work in which he is engaged (except that in everything the Lord will provide for his good), he will aim for what he thinks best, as far as he is capable. In every course of action, he will not be carried away by his own ideas, but will commit and entrust himself to God's wisdom, so that, under his guidance, he may be led into the right way. However, his confidence in outside help will not be such that its presence represents security, and its absence poverty to make him panic. His mind will always be fixed on the Providence of God alone, and nothing that happens to him will be allowed to distract his gaze. So Joab, while he acknowledges that the result of the battle is completely in God's hands, is not passive, but energetically carries out his duties. 'Be strong,' he says, 'and let us fight bravely for our people and the cities of our God. The Lord will do what is good in his sight' (2 Sam. 10:12). This same

conviction will keep us free from rashness and false confidence and will stir us to unceasing prayer. At the same time it will fill our minds with strong hope, enable us to feel secure and shout defiance to all the dangers which surround us!

10. Now we are forcibly reminded of the immeasurable blessing of thinking reverently. The tragedies which occur in this life are countless, and death comes in many guises. The body alone can harbour diseases galore, so that each man carries destruction with him, and life is interwoven with death. How could it be otherwise? Heat and cold are potential killers and everything around is a hazard with lethal power. Board a ship and you could be a plank's width from death. Mount a horse, and the stumbling of a hoof could endanger your life. Walk along the street and every tile on the roofs is a source of danger. A sharp tool in your hand, or that of a friend, could mean real possibility of injury. Every wild animal is equipped to destroy. Even in a high-walled garden, where everything is beautiful, a snake could lurk. Your house could be burnt down, to bring poverty or destruction. Your fields are subject to hail, mildew, drought and other blights which could bring devastation and famine. Then we know that poison, treachery and robbery could strike at home or abroad. In the middle of all these hazards, surely man must be extremely unhappy, like a person more dead than alive, drawing breath with difficulty, or one who has a drawn sword hanging over his head? Of course, such things don't happen very often and never all at once! I know this, but when we see things happen to others, we realise that we are no exception; they could happen to us and surely it is impossible not to be apprehensive? Can you imagine anything worse than living in such fear? It is an insult to God when we say that man, his noblest creation, is exposed to every random stroke of fortune. But of course, we were only referring to the misery which man would experience if he should be ruled by chance.

11. When once the light of divine Providence has shone in the believer's heart, he is relieved and liberated, not only from the extreme fear and anxiety which had previously oppressed him, but from all worries. Because, as he rightly rejects the idea of chance, he can confidently put himself in God's hands. What a comfort! He knows that his heavenly Father has all things in his power, directs them as he wills and rules them by his wisdom, so that nothing can happen unless he orders it. He also knows that, accepted by God's love and entrusted into his angels' care, he cannot be harmed by fire, water or weapon, unless the sovereign God allows it. So we read in the Psalm, 'Surely he will save you from the fowler's snare and from the deadly pestilence. He will cover you with his feathers, and under his wings you will find refuge; his faithfulness will be your shield and rampart. You will not fear the terror of night, nor the arrow that flies by day, nor the pestilence that stalks in the darkness, nor the plague that destroys at midday' (Ps. 91:3–6). This results in the saints' exulting confidence: 'The Lord is with me; I will not be afraid. What can man do to me? The Lord is with me; he is my helper.' 'Though an army besiege me, my heart will not fear.' 'Even though I walk through the valley of the shadow of death, I will fear no evil' (Ps. 118:6–7; 27:3; 23:4). How is it that their confidence never fails? It can only be that while the world seems to go on its random way, they know that God is at work everywhere, and they can be secure in this. When the devil and evil men attack, the believer is strengthened by remembering and thinking about Providence, otherwise he would panic. He has plenty of reasons for comfort as he realises that the devil and all the ungodly are reined in by God, so that they cannot conceive, plan or carry out any crime, unless God allows it, indeed commands it. They are not only in bondage to him, but are forced to serve him. It is the Lord's prerogative to enable the enemy's rage and to control it at will, and it is in his power to decide how far and how long it

may last, so that wicked men cannot break free and do exactly what they want ...

[12–14]

[Chapter 18]

Part V

MAN'S SIN AND GOD'S REMEDY

BOOK TWO

THE KNOWLEDGE OF GOD THE REDEEMER, IN CHRIST. THIS WAS MADE KNOWN FIRST TO THE FATHERS, IN THE LAW; AND LATER TO US IN THE GOSPEL.

Chapter 1

Through Adam's Fall and rebellion, the whole human race has been cursed and has degenerated from its original state. Original sin.

1. The old proverb which urged man to acquire the knowledge of himself was a sound one. If it is considered a shame to be ignorant of facts about life, self-ignorance is much more shameful, because it makes us deceive ourselves in matters of great importance, and so walk through life blindfold.

However, the more valuable a piece of advice is, the more careful we must be not to abuse it, as certain philosophers do. When they urge man to know himself, their motive is that he should not be ignorant of his own brilliance and position. They want to see in himself only the things which will fill him with false confidence and inflate his pride. But self-knowledge consists first of all in this: when we think of what God gave us at our birth, and still graciously continues to give, we see how splendid our nature would have been if it had been unspoilt. At the same time we remember that we have nothing of ourselves, but depend entirely on God, for whom we hold in trust whatever he sees fit to give. Secondly, when we look at our wretched state since Adam's Fall, all confidence and boasting melt away; we blush for shame and feel truly humble. God made us in his own image (Gen. 1:27), so that he might lift our minds to follow good and think of eternal life (keeping us from thoughtlessly suppressing those fine qualities which distinguish us from the lower animals). It is important to know that we were given reason and intelligence so that we might develop a holy and honest life, with the blessing of immortality as our aim. It is impossible to think of our primeval glory without being reminded at the same time of the sad spectacle of our shame and corruption ever since we fell from that first state through Adam. Thinking of this we are dissatisfied with ourselves, and become really humble. Then we are set on fire with fresh desire to seek God, in whom we may each find again those lovely qualities of which we are all completely devoid.

2. In self-examination, the search which divine truth requires and the knowledge which it demands will destroy any confidence in our own ability, leave us without any reason to boast and so lead us to submission. This is the course we must follow if we want to reach the true goal.

I am aware that a much more acceptable view encourages us to think about our good qualities, rather than dwell on our overwhelming shame and misery. The human mind loves nothing better than flattery, and so when told that its gifts are considerable, it is inclined to believe it wholeheartedly! So it is not strange that the majority of men have sinned so blatantly in this matter. Because of the innate self-love which blinds us all, we willingly convince ourselves that we do not possess a single undesirable quality. So, without any external approval, there is a general belief in the mistaken idea that man has everything he needs for a good and happy life. If some people think more modestly and give God a little credit, so that they do not appear to claim everything for themselves, the division always leaves the chief ground of confidence and boasting in themselves. Nothing is more gratifying than a speech which flatters man's innate pride. So, in every age, the one who is quickest to lift high the excellence of human nature is received with the loudest applause. Teaching man to rely on himself can be no more than sweet seduction, because everyone who is deluded by it will be ruined.

What is the point of going on in false confidence, thinking, deciding, planning and attempting what seems relevant, when, from the outset, it will prove lacking in sound wisdom and real virtue? We are merely persisting in rushing headlong to destruction, when we trust in our own ability. If we listen to teachers who get us to dwell on our good qualities, then far from making progress in self-knowledge, we will be sunk in the most disastrous ignorance.

3. While most people agree with revealed truth, in teaching that the second part of wisdom consists in self-knowledge, they differ a great deal as to how it may be acquired. By natural judgment, man considers his self-knowledge to be complete, when he boldly attempts virtuous deeds with extreme confidence in his own intelligence and integrity; or when he tries his utmost to be honourable and fair in attacking vice. However, the person who assesses himself by the standard of divine justice finds no grounds for confidence and so, the more thorough his self-examination, the greater his despair. He abandons all self-dependence and feels completely incapable of right living. But it is not God's will that we should forget the primeval dignity he gave to Adam and Eve; it may well spur us on to follow goodness and justice. We cannot think of our origins, or the end for which we were created, without having the urge to think about eternal life and to seek the kingdom of God.

Such meditation, far from encouraging us, casts us down and makes us humble. What was our original state? One from which we have fallen. What is the purpose of our creation? One from which we have wandered until, tired of our wretched lot, we groan and sigh for our lost dignity. When we say that man should find nothing in himself to raise his spirits, we mean that he has nothing to make him proud. So, in considering man's self-knowledge, it seems right to think about it like this. First, he should think about the purpose for which he was made, and the splendid qualities he was given, to spur him on to meditate on worship of God and the future life. Second, he should consider the faculties he has not got, so that when he is aware of this, all his confidence will evaporate and he will be ashamed. The effect of the first is to teach a person what his duty is, and of the second to make him realise how far he can fulfil it. We shall look at each in turn.
[4–5]

6. The contamination of parents is transmitted to their children so that everyone, without exception, is depraved from their earliest moment. The start of this depravity cannot be discovered until we go back to the first parent of all, as the fountain-head. We must grasp the fact firmly, as we think of human nature, that Adam was not just an ancestor but a root, so that by his corruption the whole human race was justly tainted. This is clear from the contrast which the apostle draws between Adam and Christ. 'Therefore, just as sin entered the world through one man, and death through sin, and in this way death came to all men, because all sinned' (Rom. 5:12), so that through Christ's grace righteousness and life are restored to us.

The Pelagians are bound to quibble over this. They might say that the sin of Adam was passed on by imitation. Is the righteousness of Christ also only available to us as an example held up for imitation? What intolerable blasphemy! But if, beyond any dispute, the righteousness of Christ and resulting life are transferred to us, it follows that both were lost in Adam that they might be regained in Christ. Sin and death were introduced by Adam, so that they might be abolished in Christ. The words are quite clear, 'For just as through the disobedience of the one man the many were made sinners, so also through the obedience of the one man the many will be made righteous' (Rom. 5:19). So the link between the two is this: as Adam, by his Fall, involved and ruined us, so Christ, by grace, restored us to salvation. In the light of this truth, I do not see the need of any further proof. Again, in the first epistle to the Corinthians, when Paul wants to strengthen believers in the sure hope of the resurrection, he shows that the life lost in Adam is recovered in Christ (1 Cor. 15:22). Having already stated that all died in Adam, he now also affirms that all are touched with the taint of sin. Condemnation could not be directed at the totally innocent! The meaning of the other half of the verse, in which he shows that the hope of life is restored in Christ, could not be clearer. Everyone knows that this can only happen when Christ transfers the power of his own righteousness to us, in the same wonderful way that 'your spirit is alive because of righteousness' (Rom. 8:10). So the only explanation of the expression 'in Adam all died', is that by sinning he not only brought disaster and ruin upon himself, but also plunged human nature into the same destruction. It was not only by one mistake, which had nothing to do with us, but by the corruption into which he fell that he infected the whole of mankind. Paul could never have said that 'we were by nature objects of wrath' (Eph. 2:3), if we had not been condemned from the womb. It is obvious that the nature referred to is not as God created it, but as it was polluted by Adam. It would be ridiculous to make God the author of death! So Adam, when he corrupted himself, passed on the contagion to all posterity. A divine Judge, our Saviour himself, states that by birth all are sinful and fallen, when he says that 'flesh gives birth to flesh' (John 3:6).

[7]

8. In case there is any confusion, it would be a good thing to define original sin. I have no intention of discussing various definitions which have been propounded, but will only argue the one which seems to agree best with the truth. Original sin, then, may be defined as the hereditary corruption and depravity of our nature. This reaches every part of the soul, makes us abhorrent to God's wrath and produces in us what Scripture calls works of the flesh. This corruption is constantly called sin by Paul (Gal. 5:19) while the things which spring from it such as adultery, fornication, theft, hatred, murder and revellings, he calls sins. Sins are the fruits of sin. The two things must be looked at separately.

First, because we are crooked and corrupt in every part of our nature, we are rightly condemned by God, who can accept nothing but righteousness, innocence and purity. This does not mean that we are being held liable for someone else's fault. When it is said that the sin of Adam has made us obnoxious to God's justice, the implication is not that we are taking his guilt, when we ourselves are innocent and blameless, but that since we are all under the curse because of his transgression, he has placed us under the debt of guilt. Through him, not only has punishment come, but pollution has been put within us so that punishment is justly due. So Augustine, though he often calls it Adam's sin, so that he may show more clearly how it came to us by descent, at the same time maintains that it is each person's own sin. The apostle very clearly states that 'death came to all men, because all sinned' (Rom. 5:12). They are involved in original sin and soiled by its stain. Even babies bring their condemnation with them from their mother's womb; they suffer for their own imperfection and no one else's. Although they have not yet produced the fruits of sin, they have the seed within. Their whole nature is like a seedbed of sin and so must be hateful and repugnant to God. It is rightly considered sinful in God's sight, because there could be no condemnation without guilt.

Now comes the second point: this perversity in us never lets up but constantly produces new fruits (those works of the flesh we referred to before), just as a burning furnace sends out sparks and flames and a fountain never ceases to pour out water. Hence, those who define original sin as the lack of the original righteousness we ought to have, though they are well on the way to understanding the situation, do not describe its power and force adequately. Our nature is not only completely empty of goodness, but so full of every kind of wrong that it is always active. Those who call it lust use an apt word, provided it is also stated (though not everyone will agree) that everything which is in man, from the intellect to the will, from the soul to the body, is defiled and imbued with this lust. To put it briefly, the whole man is in himself nothing but lust.
[9–11]

Chapter 2

Man has been deprived of free will, and is miserably enslaved.

[1–11]

12. I approve of Augustine's dictum that man's natural gifts were corrupted by sin, and his supernatural gifts withdrawn. He referred to the supernatural gifts of righteousness and the light of faith which would have enabled man to attain a place in heaven and everlasting happiness. When man withdrew his loyalty to God, he was deprived of the spiritual gifts which had lifted him to the hope of eternal salvation. So it follows that he is an exile from the kingdom of God and everything which belongs to the spiritual life is extinguished, until he regains them by the grace of regeneration. Among these are faith, love to God and neighbour

and the study of righteousness and holiness. When these are restored to us by Christ, they might be thought of as above and beyond nature. Then we infer that they were once wiped out. At the same time, soundness of mind and integrity of soul were withdrawn and it is this which produces the corruption of natural gifts. Although there is a residue of intelligence and judgment as well as will, a mind which is weak and darkened cannot be called sound and whole. The depravity of the will is only too well known. So, since reason, by which man discerns between good and evil and by which he understands and judges, is a natural gift, it could not be completely destroyed. But because it was weakened and corrupted to some extent, only a shapeless wreck is left. In this sense we read in John 1:5: 'The light shines in the darkness, but the darkness has not understood it.' These words clearly express both aspects. First, that there are still some sparks in man's perverted and degenerate nature which show that he is a rational animal. He differs from the lower orders because he possesses intelligence, but the light of it is enveloped in dark clouds so that it cannot shine out effectively. In the same way, because the will is inseparable from man's nature, it did not perish, but became so bound by depraved lusts as to be incapable of worthy desires.

I have now completed my definition but several points need explanation. In line with the division of the soul into intellect and will, we must now study the power of the intellect. It is contrary to the Word of God and to common experience to maintain that the intellect is for ever blind, with no capacity at all. A longing to investigate the truth has been implanted in the human mind, and it would never rise to this unless some appetite for truth had existed from the beginning. There is discernment in the human mind to this extent, that it is naturally influenced by the love of truth: the neglect of this in the lower animals is proof of their base unreasoning nature. However, this love of truth fades out before it reaches the goal and then falls away into vanity.

Because the human mind is unable, through obtuseness, to follow the right line of enquiry, after various attempts and stumbling from time to time like a person groping in the dark, it eventually gets utterly confused. This just proves how unfit the mind is to search for the truth and to find it. It labours under another serious defect, in that it often fails to discern what sort of knowledge it should try to acquire. So, influenced by mere curiosity, it tortures itself with unnecessary and useless discussion, either not referring at all to essential matters or giving them only a superficial and contemptuous glance. It hardly ever studies them with serious purpose. Secular writers constantly complain about this futile approach and yet almost all of them do the same! So Solomon, throughout the book of Ecclesiastes, lists all the areas in which men think they are wisest and then pronounces them futile and frivolous.
[13–17]

18. We must now explain what the power of human reason is in relation to the kingdom of God; also spiritual discernment which consists mainly of three things. These are the knowledge of God, the knowledge of his fatherly love towards us in which our salvation consists and the way in which we can run our lives in tune with the Law of God. As to the first two (and especially the second) the cleverest of men are blinder than moles. I do not dispute that in some philosophical writings we occasionally come across some wise and relevant comments on the nature of God, but they are invariably tinged with confused fantasies. The Lord has given such philosophers a slight awareness of his Godhead, so that they cannot plead ignorance as an excuse for blasphemy. At times he has prompted them to proclaim their views in such a way as to be their own condemnation. Seeing, they saw not. Their discernment was not enough to lead them to the truth, far less to grasp it: it was like that of a confused traveller seeing his surroundings momentarily by a flash of lightning, and then disappearing before he can

move a step. Such assistance can never help him to find the right path. Many wicked lies get mixed up with the tiny particles of truth in the writings of these philosophers. Not one made the slightest contribution to the assurance of divine favour, without which man's mind will always remain in the chaos of confusion. Human reason cannot begin to answer the great questions as to what God is in himself, and what he is in relation to us.
[19–27]

Chapter 3

Everything proceeding from the corrupt nature of man is damnable.

[1–2]

3. Now we have a problem to solve. In every age there have been people who, by nature, wanted to lead good lives. Of course, many faults could be found in their behaviour, but simply by following virtue they showed the element of purity in their characters. Such examples keep us from thinking that the nature of man is totally evil, since some have been outstanding in noble acts as well as behaving with integrity throughout their lives. We must realise that, despite our fallen natures, there is room for divine grace. This grace will restrain the heart inwardly without cleansing it. If the Lord allowed every mind to do exactly what it wanted, it is quite certain that each of us would show our nature to be capable of every crime Paul mentions. Tell me, are you completely innocent of murder and theft? Don't your lips speak deceitful, spiteful things? Aren't your actions often wrong and harmful? Our souls are without God; our inmost beings are sinful; we are devious and malevolent with every part of us capable of lifelong evil (Rom. 3:10–18). If we are all like this (and the apostle says so clearly), it is easy to see

what would happen if the Lord allowed human passion to have its way. No wild beast would rush with such fury, no stream, however rapid and turbulent, would burst its banks so boisterously. God heals the elect of these evil things; others he only restrains so that they do not break out in a way which makes it impossible to maintain law and order.

However much such people disguise their sinfulness, some are held back from action only by shame, others by fear of the law. Some try to live an honest life, thinking it to be in their own interest, while others rise above common folk, so that by dignity of rank they can keep inferior folk in their place. So God, by his Providence, curbs the perversity of nature, preventing it from breaking out in action, but not making it inwardly pure.

4. We haven't yet answered the objection, however. Either we must equate the notorious evil-doer Cataline with the particularly noble patriot Camillus, or maintain that Camillus is an illustration of the truth that nature, carefully nurtured, has some good in it. I admit that the flattering qualities which Camillus possessed were divine gifts, and seem very commendable. But how are they proofs of a virtuous nature? Surely we have to go back to the mind and reason like this: If a natural man possesses real integrity, his nature is capable of pursuing virtue. But what if his mind is depraved and perverted, following anything but good? That was the case with Camillus, if we agree that he was only a natural man. How can we praise the power of human nature to do good, when, even in the best, a corrupt bias is discernible? So, just as you would not commend a man for virtue, when his vices harm you under the cloak of virtue, so you must not attribute the power of choosing aright to the will while it is rooted in depravity. The surest and easiest answer to the objection is that these are not general gifts of nature, but special gifts of God, which he distributes in different forms and definite measure to men who are sinful in other respects. So in everyday speech we say that one man

is good and another bad, but we must also maintain that both are depraved like everyone else. God has given one special grace which he has not seen fit to confer on the other. When he chose to set Saul over the kingdom, it was as if he made him a new man (1 Sam. 10:6). This is what Plato meant when he referred to a passage in the *Iliad* and said that the children of royalty are distinguished at birth by some special qualities. God, in his kindness to the human race, often gives a spirit of heroism to those he destines for leadership. It was in this way that famous leaders of the past were born, and the same must be said for ordinary mortals. But those with the greatest gifts are always driven by the strongest ambition (a fault which spoils every virtue and makes it unacceptable to God); so there is no value in anything that appears praiseworthy in ungodly men. The most important part of integrity is lacking when there is no zeal for God's glory, and there is no such zeal in those who are not born again of the Spirit. Isaiah says with good reason that on Christ would rest 'the Spirit of knowledge and of the fear of the Lord' (Isa. 11:2); for we learn from this that all who are strangers to Christ are without the fear of God which is the beginning of wisdom (Ps. 111:10). The virtues which deceive us may be acclaimed in society and daily life, but before God's judgment seat they will be useless in establishing a claim to righteousness.

5. When the will is enslaved by sin, it cannot start to be good, let alone maintain good ways. But every attempt is the first step towards conversion, which is entirely due to God's grace. So Jeremiah prays, 'Restore me, and I will return' (Jer. 31:18). In the same chapter, describing the spiritual redemption of believers, he says, 'For the Lord will ransom Jacob and will redeem them from the hand of those stronger than they' (Jer. 31:11). This shows how strong the fetters are which bind the sinner, as long as he is away from the Lord and under the devil's sway. Man's will urges him on to love sin passionately, and when he is bound

by it he will be deprived not of his will but a healthy will. Bernard says rightly that we all have a will: to use it well means success, to use it badly failure. Simply to will is common to all men; to will evil is the work of a corrupt nature and to will good the work of grace. The enslaved will is inevitably drawn to evil. This idea seems to offend those who cannot distinguish between necessity and coercion. If anyone asked them 'Isn't God necessarily good? Isn't the devil necessarily wicked?' What answer would they give? The goodness of God is so linked with his Godhead that it is not more necessary to be God than to be good; whereas the devil by his fall was so cut off from goodness, that he can do nothing but evil.

If anyone makes the irreverent remark that little credit can be given to God for enforced goodness, surely one has to reply that it is not because of coercion, but because of his boundless goodness, that he cannot do evil? So, if God's free will in doing good is not constricted because he necessarily must do good, and if the devil, who can do nothing but evil, nevertheless sins voluntarily, can it be said that man sins less voluntarily because he necessarily sins? Augustine consistently teaches this necessity. Even when criticised by Celestius, he maintains that 'Man became a sinner through his freedom, but corruption, which followed as the penalty, changed freedom into necessity'.

Whenever the subject is mentioned Augustine does not hesitate to speak in this way of the inevitable bondage of sin. So let us sum up the distinction. Since man was corrupted by the Fall, he sins voluntarily. There is no external force or coercion: he is motivated by his own passions. But such is the depravity of his nature, he can only move in the direction of evil. Bernard, agreeing with Augustine, writes,

> In the animal world, man alone is free. Because sin has intervened, he suffers a kind of violence, but this comes from his will, not from nature, so that it does not deprive him of innate freedom.

What is voluntary must be free. Then he adds:

> In some strange and evil manner, the will itself, under-mined by sin, imposes a necessity upon itself. But the necessity, being voluntary, cannot excuse the will, and the will, being led astray, cannot escape the necessity.

This necessity is as it were voluntary. Later he says:

> We are under a yoke of voluntary bondage. As regards bondage, we are miserable, and as regards will, inexcus-able, because the will, when it was free, made itself the slave of sin.

Finally he concludes:

> So the soul, in some strange and evil way, is held under this kind of voluntary, yet sadly free necessity, both bond and free. It is enslaved because of the necessity, and free because it is a will. What is stranger and sadder still, it is guilty because free, and enslaved because guilty, therefore enslaved because free.

So my readers will see that the doctrine I pass on is not new, but one which Augustine set forth with the agreement of all the saints. It was guarded in the monasteries for nearly a thousand years. Peter Lombard gave rise to a dangerous error because he could not distinguish between necessity and coercion.

6. It would be right to think about the remedy divine grace provides for correction and curing natural corruption. The Lord, in coming to our aid, gives us what we need and thereby reveals our helplessness. When the apostle says to the Philippians, 'being confident of this, that he who began a good work in you will carry it on to completion until the day of Christ Jesus' (Phil. 1:6), there can be no doubt that

by the good work begun he means the first step of conversion in the will. So God begins the good work in us by arousing in our hearts a desire, love and study of righteousness. More accurately, he turns, trains and guides our hearts to righteousness. He completes the good work by strengthening us to keep going to the end. In case anyone tries to quibble that the good work done by the Lord consists in helping the will (which is weak in itself), the Spirit states what the will is able to do on its own. 'I will give you a new heart and put a new spirit in you; I will remove from you your heart of stone and give you a heart of flesh. And I will put my Spirit in you and move you to follow my decrees and be careful to keep my laws' (Ezek. 36:26–7). How can it be said that the weakness of the human will is merely assisted effectively to choose good things, when in fact it must be totally transformed and renewed? If there is any softness in a stone or you can make it malleable, then you could say that the human heart could be reshaped correctly, so long as the imperfect is assisted by divine grace. If the Spirit intends to show that no good thing can ever be drawn from our hearts, unless they are made new, we must not try to share with him what he claims for himself alone.

If it is like turning a stone into flesh, when God gets us to follow the right way, everything belonging to our own will is abolished, and what succeeds is wholly of him. I say the will is abolished, but not in so far as it is will, for in conversion everything essential to our old nature remains. When I say that the will is created anew, it is not because it then begins to exist, but because it is turned from evil to good. I maintain that this is totally God's work, because as the apostle teaches, 'Not that we are competent to claim anything for ourselves' (2 Cor. 3:5). In Philippians 2:13 he says not merely that God helps the weak or corrects the depraved will, but that he works in us to will. From this we can infer that everything good in the will is entirely the result of grace. In the same way the apostle says, 'There are different kinds of working, but the same God works all of them

in all men' (1 Cor. 12:6). He is not referring to universal government, but stating that all the good qualities which believers possess are due to God. In using the term 'all', he definitely makes God the Author of spiritual life from beginning to end. He explained this in different terms when he said that 'there is but one Lord, Jesus Christ, through whom all things come and through whom we live' (1 Cor. 8:6). Here he plainly extols the new creation, by which everything in our common nature is destroyed. There is a tacit antithesis between Adam and Christ, which he explains more clearly when he says 'For we are God's workmanship, created in Christ Jesus to do good works, which God prepared in advance for us to do' (Eph. 2:10). He shows in this way that our salvation is gratuitous, because the beginning of goodness is from the second creation, obtained in Christ. If we had the slightest ability in ourselves, there would be merit. But to show our complete destitution, he argues that we merit nothing because we are created in Christ Jesus to do good works, which God has prepared. He implies by these words that all the fruits of good works are straight from God. So the Psalmist, after saying that the Lord has made us, immediately adds 'not we ourselves', to take from us any share in the work. It is obvious from the context that he is referring to regeneration, the beginning of spiritual life, because his next words are, 'we are his people, the sheep of his pasture' (Ps. 100:3). Not content with simply giving God the glory for our salvation, he specifically excludes us from any part in it. Man has not an atom of cause to boast. The whole work is God's.
[7–9]

10. For many years there was teaching about God's work in the will, which said that man was left the option of obeying or resisting it. We are speaking about something different which affects us efficaciously. We must repudiate Chrysostom's statement 'Whom he draws, he draws as they are willing', which implies that the Lord merely stretches out his

hand and then waits to see whether we choose to accept his help. We agree that, as man was originally created, he could incline either way, but since experience shows how miserable free will is if God does not work in us to will and act, what use is such a slight measure of grace? By our own ingratitude, we cover up and weaken divine grace. The apostle's doctrine is not that the gift of a good will is offered to us if we will accept it, but that God himself is pleased to work in us so as to guide, steer and rule our hearts by his Spirit, and reign there as his property. Ezekiel promises that a new spirit will be given to the elect, not merely that they may be able to walk in his ways, but that they may actually do so (Ezek. 11:19; 36:27). The meaning of our Saviour's words 'Everyone who listens to the Father and learns from him comes to me' (John 6:45), must be that the grace of God is effectual in itself. Augustine agrees with this in his book *The Predestination of the Saints*. This grace is not given to everyone indiscriminately; according to Occam's maxim it is not refused to anyone who does his best. Men must indeed be taught that God's favour is offered, without exception, to all who ask for it, but since only those who are inspired by God's grace do ask, every particle of praise must go to him. It is the privilege of the elect to be born again by God's Spirit, and then placed under his guidance and rule. So Augustine rightly scorns those who presume that they have the power of willing, and also condemns others who imagine that something which is a special sign of gratuitous election is given to everyone. He says, 'Nature is common to all, but grace is not.' In another place he says: 'How did you come to God? By believing. Watch out that you don't fall from the right way, by claiming merit for finding it yourself. I came, you say, by free choice, by my own will. Why do you boast? Don't you know that even this was a gift? Listen to Christ exclaiming "No-one can come to me, unless the Father who sent me draws him" (John 6:44).' From the words of John he infers that the hearts of believers are so effectually controlled by God, that they respond with undeviating love. 'No-one who is born of God will continue to sin, because God's seed remains in him' (1 John 3:9). The intermediate movement of the will which some theologians devise, where everyone is free to obey or to reject, is obviously excluded by the doctrine of effectual perseverance.

[11–14]

[Chapters 4–5]

Part VI

GOD'S LAW

Chapter 6

Redemption for fallen man is to be sought in Christ.

1. Because the whole human race was ruined in the person of Adam – the splendour of our origin, far from being to our benefit, added to our disgrace – until God (who does not acknowledge man corrupted by sin as his work) appeared as redeemer in the person of his only begotten Son. Since the Fall, all our knowledge of God the Creator would be useless unless it led to faith in God as Father in Christ. This present world should be the school where we learn godliness, and then pass on to eternal life and perfect bliss. But though we see perfection wherever we look, our hearts are filled with despair when we realise that divine judgment rests on us and all affected by our sin. Although God graciously shows his fatherly goodness to us in many ways, we cannot infer that he is a Father simply by looking at the world. Conscience is at work in us, telling us that we deserve to be rejected because of sin, and not allowing us to imagine that God thinks of us as sons. Then there is our laziness and ingratitude. Our minds are blinded so that they cannot see the truth, and our senses are so corrupt that we shamefully rob God of his glory. So we must conclude with Paul, 'since in the wisdom of God the world through its wisdom did not know him, God was pleased through the foolishness of what was preached to save those who believe' (1 Cor. 1:21). By the 'wisdom of God' he means the magnificent arena of heaven and earth, filled with countless amazing things which should enable us to know God if we observed them aright. But we don't, and so he invites us to

faith in Christ. This faith seems foolish to the unbeliever and so disgusts him. So, although the preaching of the cross does not square with human wisdom, we must accept it humbly if we want to return to God our Maker (from whom we are estranged) so that he may become our Father again. After the Fall of Adam, no knowledge of God could save us without a mediator. Christ does not speak only of his own age, but embraces all ages when he says, 'This is eternal life: that they may know you, the only true God, and Jesus Christ, whom you have sent' (John 17:3). This makes quite inexcusable the presumption of those who throw heaven open to the unbeliever, without the grace which Scripture describes as the only door into eternal life. If anyone tries to restrict our Saviour's words to the time of the Gospel, it is not difficult to prove them wrong. We find clear proclamation that in every age and nation, all who are estranged from God and so are under the curse as children of wrath, cannot please him until they are reconciled. There is also the reply our Saviour gave to the Samaritan woman 'You Samaritans worship what you do not know; we worship what we do know, for salvation is from the Jews' (John 4:22). In these words he makes every Gentile religion false because under the Law the redeemer was promised to the chosen people alone; so worship could be pleasing to God only if it looked to Christ. Paul maintains that all the Gentiles were 'without God' and without the hope of eternal life (Eph. 2:12). Now, since John teaches that there was life in Christ from the beginning, and that the whole world had lost it (John 1:1–14), we must return to that fountain. Here Christ declares that because he is propitiator, he is life. Indeed, only the sons of God have heaven as their inheritance. It would be quite incongruous to give the status of sons to any who have not been grafted into the body of God's only begotten Son. John plainly states that those who believe in his name become the sons of God (John 1:12). [2–4]

Chapter 7

The Law was given to the Jews not as an end in itself but to keep alive hope of salvation in Christ until his coming.

[1–2]

3. In order that a sense of guilt may spur us on to seek for forgiveness, it is important to know how instruction in the moral Law makes us more culpable. If it is true that perfect righteousness is set out in the Law, it follows that complete obedience to it would mean absolute righteousness in God's sight. So Moses, after proclaiming the Law, does not hesitate to call heaven and earth to witness that he had set life and death, good and evil before the people. We know that the reward of eternal salvation, as promised by the Lord, would await perfect obedience to the Law (Deut. 30:19). It is important to understand how we can obey and have hope of that reward. It is no good seeing that eternal life depends on keeping the Law, unless we try to discover whether that is possible. Here then, the weakness of the Law is demonstrated: righteousness can be seen in none of us and so, cut off from the promise of life, we fall under the curse. I am stating not only what happens but what inevitably happens. The requirements of the Law are beyond us, and so a man may see the promises held from a distance, but he will never benefit from them. All he can do is get a clearer picture of his own misery by comparison with their loveliness, while he realises that the hope of salvation is cut off and certain death hangs over him. The terrible pronouncements which are directed at us all rise up and with relentless severity follow us. Nothing but instant death is offered by the Law.

4. So if we look only to the Law, the result will be depres-

sion, confusion and hopelessness, since we are all de-
nounced and condemned by it, and kept at a distance from
the happiness offered to any who could obey it fully. You
may well ask if the Lord is playing games with us! It seems
almost mockery to hold out the hope of happiness, to invite
and urge us on towards it, to underline its reality, while all
the time the gateway is barred and locked. My answer is
this: although the promises are conditional on perfect
obedience of the Law and this does not exist, they have not
been given in vain. When we have realised that the promises are empty and useless, unless God accepts us by free
grace, without reference to our works, and when, having
realised this, we claim by faith the grace offered in the Gospel, the promises with all their implications are wonderfully
fulfilled. God gives us everything freely and crowns his
goodness by not scorning our faulty obedience. He forgives
its imperfections and accepts it as though it were complete,
so granting us everything the Law has promised.

5. ... If we go back as far as possible in history, we shall not
find a mortal soul who loved the Lord with all his heart and
soul, mind and strength, and not one who has not experienced the power of lust. Who could deny this? I know there
are saints, imagined by the superstitious to be almost equal
in purity with the angels. But this is contrary to Scripture
and experience. No saint will ever be perfect, as long as he
lives. Scripture bears clear testimony to this, 'for there is
no-one who does not sin' (1 Kgs 8:46). David says, 'for no-
one living is righteous before you' (Ps. 143:2). Job too, in
several places, asserts the same thing. But the plainest of all
is Paul who declares that 'the sinful nature desires what is
contrary to the Spirit, and the Spirit what is contrary to the
sinful nature' (Gal. 5:17) ...

6. To make things even clearer, let us take a concentrated
look at the purpose and use of the moral Law. It seems to
consist of three parts. First, by displaying the righteousness

of God, it rebukes everyone for his own unrighteousness, puts him on trial, convicts and finally condemns him. This is necessary so that man, who is blind and smitten with love of himself, may be brought to know and confess his weakness and impurity. Until his vanity is exposed, he is puffed up with infatuated pride in his own abilities. He will never be aware of their limitations as long as he measures them by a standard of his own choice. As soon as he begins to compare them with the demands of the Law his presumption is cut down to size. However high his opinion of his own powers might be, he realises how inadequate they are as they falter and finally collapse under him. The one who is disciplined by the Law gets rid of the arrogance which previously blinded him. In the same way, he must be cured of pride, the other disease from which he suffers. As long as he is allowed to appeal to his own judgment, he puts a hypocritical righteousness in place of the genuine and, quite happy with this, he creates false practices which conflict with God's grace. After he is made to weigh his behaviour in the balance of the Law, renouncing any dependence on an imagined righteousness, he sees how very far he is from true holiness, and that he is full of countless vices he was unaware of before. The corners in which lust gets hidden are so deep and twisted that they easily escape our vision. So the apostle had good reason for saying 'I would not have known lust, unless the law had said "You shall not covet"' (Rom. 7:7). If it is not brought out of its hiding-place, it treacherously destroys in secret before its fatal sting is discovered.

7. The Law is a kind of mirror. When we look in the mirror we notice any dirty marks on our faces, so in the Law we are made aware first of our helplessness, then of our sin and finally the judgment. This is an inevitable sequence. The greater the sin of which the Law convicts us, the stricter the judgment meted out to us. The apostle agrees with this when he says, 'through the law we become conscious of sin'

(Rom. 3:20). In these words he underlines the primary job of the Law as experienced by the unregenerate. He makes the same point again: 'The law was added so that the trespass might increase' and that it is 'the ministry that brought death' and that it 'brings wrath' (Rom. 5:20; 2 Cor. 3:7; Rom. 4:15). There is no doubt that the more awareness there is of guilt, the more sin there is, because a sense of rebellion against the Lawgiver creeps in. All that the Law can do then is to prepare God's wrath for the destruction of the sinner. On its own it can only accuse, condemn and destroy. So Augustine says 'If the Spirit of grace is absent, the law is present only to convict and kill.' To say this is not to insult the Law, nor detract from its excellence. Indeed, if our wills were inclined to obedience, the mere knowledge of the Law would be enough for salvation. But since our unregenerate nature is at enmity with the divine Law, and is in no way made right by its discipline, it becomes the cause of death rather than life. When everyone is convicted of sin, the more the Law proclaims God's righteousness and exposes our iniquity. The more it assures us of life and salvation as the reward of the righteous, the more clearly it confirms that the unrighteous will perish. Far from bringing the Law into disrepute, all this makes God's goodness shine the brighter. It shows that it is only our weakness and depravity that prevent us from enjoying the happiness which the Law offers. So divine grace is made even sweeter: it comes to our aid without the Law. God's mercy is made even lovelier because it proclaims that he is never weary of doing good and showering us with gifts.

8. While the Law affirms universal sin and condemnation, it does not follow that we must give up hope and be plunged into despair. It may have this effect on the ungodly because of their obstinacy. With the children of God it is different. The apostle confirms that the Law pronounces sentence of condemnation in order 'that every mouth may be silenced and the whole world held accountable to God' (Rom.

3:19). In another place, however, he declares that 'God has bound all men over to disobedience' not that he might destroy everyone but that 'he may have mercy on them all' (Rom. 11:32). In other words, when we discard the ridiculously high opinion we have of our own virtue, we can see how totally dependent we are on God's help. When we see how poverty-stricken we are, we take refuge in his mercy, rely upon it and find complete protection. We renounce all goodness and merit of our own and hold on to God's mercy alone, offered in Christ to all who long and look for it with his faith. In the maxims of the Law, God is seen as the rewarder of perfect righteousness and the avenger of sin. But in Christ, his face shines out, full of grace and gentleness to poor, unworthy sinners.
[9]

10. The second function of the Law is to control those who would have no concern for just and right behaviour, unless there was fear of punishment. Such people are controlled, not because their thinking is affected, but because (as though a rein was holding them in) they refrain from outward action and inwardly check the viciousness which would otherwise burst out. True, they are neither better nor more righteous in God's sight because of this. It is only because restrained by fear or shame that they dare not act on impulse, nor give way to raging lust; not because their hearts are disciplined to be obedient. In fact, the more they restrain themselves, the more angry they get, ready to break out in any direction, if it were not for the threat of the Law. Not only this, they thoroughly detest the Law itself, and loathe the Lawgiver. If they could, they would gladly wipe him off the face of the earth, because they cannot bear his commands to do right and his punishment of those who rebel. The feeling of all those who are not yet regenerate is that they are dragged by force of fear to obey the Law, not by voluntary submission. Nevertheless, this enforced good behaviour is essential for the good of society, otherwise ev-

erything would be thrown into confusion. And this discipline is valuable even for the children of God. Before their effectual calling, they too were without the Spirit of holiness and freely indulged the lusts of the flesh. When, by fear of divine retribution, they were deterred from open sin, they were to some extent trained to bear the yoke of righteousness. So when God calls them to himself, they already have some experience of righteousness to build on. This function seems to be especially in the apostle's mind when he said,

> that law is made not for good men but for lawbreakers and rebels, the ungodly and sinful, the unholy and irreligious; for those who kill their fathers or mothers, for murderers, for adulterers and perverts, for slave traders and liars and perjurers – and for whatever else is contrary to the sound doctrine (1 Tim. 1:9–10).

So he indicates clearly that the Law is a restraint on lust that would otherwise burst all bonds.
[11]

12. The third function of the Law (which is the main one and most closely connected with its ultimate purpose) refers to believers in whose hearts God's Spirit already reigns. Although the Law is written in their hearts by God and they are so influenced by his Spirit that they want to obey him, there are two ways in which they can still profit by the Law. It is the best means for them to learn daily, with greater certainty, what the will of the Lord is which they long to follow. The servant who longs with all his heart to please his master must observe his inclinations and try to give satisfaction. We must do the same, for none of us has acquired such wisdom that we cannot move on to a clearer knowledge of God's will by daily teaching from the Law. We don't need doctrine alone, but encouragement, which can also be gained from the Law. As we meditate on it fre-

quently, we shall be spurred on to obey and be drawn back
from the slippery paths of sin. In this way the saints must
press on. However eager they are, under the Spirit's control, to hurry on to righteousness, they are held back by the
sluggishness of the flesh and make slow progress. The Law
acts as a whip, urging a man on like a lazy donkey! Even
with a spiritual man, as he is still weighed down by sins of
the flesh, the Law is a constant stimulus, spurring him on
when he would like to let up. David was thinking of this
when he praised the Law like this: 'The law of the Lord is
perfect, reviving the soul. The statutes of the Lord are
trustworthy, making wise the simple. The precepts of the
Lord are right, giving joy to the heart. The commands of
the Lord are radiant, giving light to the eyes' (Ps. 19:7–8).
And again, 'Your word is a lamp to my feet and a light for
my path' (Ps. 119:105). The whole Psalm is full of similar
statements. In a similar way Paul speaks of the benefits of
the Law. The Psalmist's aim is to celebrate the advantages
which the Lord, by means of his Law, gives to those whom
he inspires to obedience. He not only refers to the commands but also to the promises linked with them, to make
the bitter sweet. The Law merely repels us, when by its
harsh demands it fills our soul with terror. David shows
clearly that he saw the Mediator in the Law; without him it
could hold no pleasure or delight.
[13–17]

Chapter 8

Exposition of the moral Law.

1. I think it would be appropriate now to introduce the Ten
Commandments of the Law, and give a brief exposition. It
will then be clearer that the homage God originally called
for is still required. A second point will emerge: the Jews
not only learned from the Law what constituted true holi-

ness, but, being aware of their inability to keep it, they were drawn, by fear of judgment and against their will, to the Mediator. In summarising what constitutes true knowledge of God, we showed that we cannot form a true picture of his character without feeling awed by his majesty and compelled to serve him. As to knowledge of ourselves, we showed that it consists mainly of renouncing any idea of our own strength, and throwing away all confidence in our own righteousness. So, made fully aware of our need, we learn true humility. The Lord accomplishes this by his Law, first when by asserting the right he has to our obedience, he calls us to reverence his majesty and show it by our life style. Second, in proclaiming his rule of justice, he charges us with inability and unrighteousness. This is because our nature, being fallen and twisted, is constantly opposed to the purity of his Law, and, being weak and cowardly, is worlds away from fulfilling it. Further, the very things contained in the tables of the Law are spelled out to us by that inner law which is written in our hearts. Instead of letting us stifle our awareness and sleep on, conscience acts as an internal witness, reminding us of our debt to God, pointing out the difference between good and evil, and convicting us of failing in our duty. Because man is imprisoned in the darkness of error, he is hardly able, by means of the natural law, to form any reasonable idea of worship which is acceptable to God. In addition, he is so puffed up with arrogance and ambition, and so blinded with love of self, that he cannot look into himself and so learn to be humble and confess his wretchedness. So, as a remedy for our obtuseness and disobedience, the Lord has given us his written Law, which removes the obscurity of the law of nature by its definite statements. Also, by raising us from lethargy it makes a more vivid and lasting impression on our minds.

2. It is now easy to understand the doctrine of the Law: that God, as our Creator, is entitled to be thought of as Father and Master and so should receive from us awe, love, rever-

ence and worship. We are not our own, to do whatever our desires dictate, but must obey him implicitly and agree to everything he asks. The Law teaches that justice and integrity are pleasing to him, and injustice is abhorrent. So if we do not want to rebel against our Maker with flagrant ingratitude, we must spend our whole lives in following righteousness. Since we can show due reverence only when we prefer his way to ours, it is obvious that we serve correctly only where we practise justice, purity and holiness. We cannot plead as an excuse that we lack the power and, like debtors without any means, find ourselves unable to pay. We must never measure God's glory by our ability. Whatever we may be he remains the same, the friend of righteousness and the enemy of unrighteousness. Whatever his demands on us may be, because he can only ask what is right, we are obviously bound to obey. Our inability to do so is our own fault. If lust, where sin holds sway, grips us in such a way that we are not free to obey our Father because the evil necessity comes from within, we must be at fault.

3. When we have reached this point, under the guidance of the Law, we must go on to look into our own hearts under the same guidance. We shall arrive at two conclusions. First as we contrast our conduct with the righteousness of the Law, we see how very far it is from agreeing with God's will. We realise how unworthy we are of being his creatures at all, let alone being regarded as sons. Second, as we assess our powers, we see that they are not only inadequate for fulfilling the Law, but good for nothing. The result of all this is to produce distrust of our own ability and also an anxious and fearful mind. Conscience cannot feel the burden of guilt without turning to God's judgment; this brings with it the fear of death. In the same way, evidence of our complete powerlessness makes us despair of our own strength. Both feelings produce humility and shame, so the sinner, terrified at the prospect of eternal death (which he sees hanging over him rightly for his sin), turns to God's mercy

as the only safe refuge. Realising his total inability to pay what he owes the Law, and so despairing of himself, he looks to some other quarter for help.

4. The Lord is not satisfied with merely inspiring respect for his justice. To fill our hearts with love for himself and with hatred for sin, he has added promises and warnings. Because the eyes of our minds are too dim to be attracted simply by the beauty of goodness, our gracious Father has seen fit, in his great mercy, to lead us on to love and long for it by the hope of reward. So he makes clear that rewards for virtue are treasured up with him. No one who obeys his commands will labour in vain. On the other hand, he declares that he hates sin, and that it will not escape unpunished because he will avenge any insult to his sovereignty. To encourage us in every way, he promises blessings in this life as well as everlasting joy to all who obey his commands, but he warns transgressors of present suffering as well as eternal death. The promise 'Keep my decrees and laws, for the man who obeys them will live by them' (Lev. 18:5) and a corresponding warning, 'The soul who sins is the one who will die' (Ezek. 18:4, 20), undoubtedly indicate a future life and death, both endless. In every passage where the favour or anger of God is mentioned, the first includes eternal life and the second eternal destruction. At the same time the Law enumerates a long list of present blessings and adversities (Lev. 26:4; Deut. 28:1–14). The warnings affirm God's absolute purity which cannot bear sin, while the promises affirm his infinite love of righteousness (which he cannot leave unrewarded) and his amazing kindness. Because we are bound to pay him homage with everything we possess, he is perfectly entitled to demand everything he wants of us as his due. Because it is his due, payment doesn't deserve a reward. So when he offers a reward for service we cannot offer spontaneously, but only as his due, he is giving up his right. The promises of the Law are clear approval of righteousness, as they show how

much God is pleased when they are kept. The warnings are intended to produce greater hatred of sin, in case the sinner succumbs to the attractions of vice and forgets the judgment which the divine Lawgiver has prepared.
[5]

6. When we have expounded the divine Law, what has already been said about its function will be easier to understand. Before we look at each commandment separately, it would be good to make a survey of the whole. It was proved at the outset that in the Law men are instructed in inner righteousness, not merely outward behaviour. No one can deny this, but very few take any notice because they pay no attention to the Lawgiver, whose character determines the nature of the Law. If a king issued an edict forbidding murder, adultery and theft, the punishment would not fall on a man who longed to commit the crime, but had not done so. A human lawgiver is concerned with outward behaviour, so his commands are defied only in actions. But God, who sees everything, and who looks for purity of heart rather than outward show, includes anger, hatred, lust and covetousness and many other things when he forbids murder, adultery and theft. Being a spiritual Lawgiver, he speaks to the soul as much as the body. The murder which the soul commits is anger and hatred; the theft is envy and greed; the adultery is lust. You may say that human laws are concerned with intentions and wishes, not chance happenings. I agree, but these have to manifest themselves externally. Such laws take into account the intention with which the act was done, but do not scrutinise the secret thoughts. So their demands are satisfied when the hand merely holds back from crime. By contrast, the Law of heaven is implemented for our minds, and the first requirement to bring about observance of the Law is to bring them under control. Most men, when they are concerned to hide their flouting of the Law, merely bring their bodily action into line. Meanwhile their hearts are completely cut off from obedience. They

think it is enough to hide from men what they are doing before God. When they hear the commands 'You shall not
kill', 'You shall not commit adultery' and 'You shall not
steal', they do not draw swords to kill, nor defile their
bodies with prostitutes, nor go out and grab other people's
belongings. So far, so good. But with their whole being,
they breathe out murder, boil with lust and cast a greedy
eye at their neighbour's property. The principal requirement of the Law is missing. They lose sight of the Lawgiver
and form their own idea of righteousness to suit themselves. How stupid can you be? Paul strongly objects when
he declares that the 'law is spiritual' (Rom. 7:14). He
suggests that the Law demands not only homage of soul,
mind and will, but a perfect purity which, cleansed from
sins of the flesh, savours only of the Spirit.
[7–50]

51. It is not hard now to discover the purpose of the whole
Law. It is the fulfilment of righteousness, so that men may
model their lives on the example of divine purity. God has
outlined his own character in the Law in such a way that
anyone who carries out his commands would to some extent portray a living image of God. So Moses, when he
wanted to impress the whole Law in the Israelites'
memories, said to them 'And now, O Israel, what does the
Lord your God ask of you but to fear the Lord your God,
to walk in all his ways, to love him, to serve the Lord your
God with all your heart and with all your soul, and to observe the Lord's commands and decrees that I am giving
you today for your own good?' (Deut. 10:12–13). He constantly repeated this, whenever he had occasion to mention
the purpose of the Law. The doctrine of the Law stresses
the connection of man to God by holiness of life. As Moses
states, it makes him cleave to God (Deut. 6:5; 11:13). This
holiness of life is summarised thus: '"Love the Lord your
God with all your heart and with all your soul and with all
your strength and with all your mind"; and "Love your

neighbour as yourself"' (Luke 10:27).

First, our minds must be completely filled with love to God, and then this love must flow out to our neighbours. The apostle says the same: 'The goal of this command is love, which comes from a pure heart and a good conscience and a sincere faith' (1 Tim. 1:5). Conscience and genuine faith come first; in other words, true godliness. Brotherly love springs from it. It is wrong to imagine that only the basics and first principles of righteousness are given in the Law, to create a kind of introduction to good works and not to lead on to a perfect fulfilment. Nothing more is needed for complete perfection than is expressed in these passages from Moses and Paul. How much more could one ask than instructions which lead man to the fear of God, to spiritual worship and practical obedience – in short, a pure conscience, a genuine faith and practical love? Those who simply search for sterile fragments, as if the Law could only teach half the will of God, fail to understand its purpose, as the apostle shows.
[52–53]

54. Our lives will harmonise best with God's will and the demands of his Law when they serve other people best. There is not a syllable in the Law which gives a ruling as to what a man must do or not do for the advantage of his own carnal nature. Since men tend to excessive love of self, no law is needed to encourage such love. So it is quite obvious that obeying the commandments does not consist in loving ourselves, but in loving God and our neighbour. The one who leads the best and holiest life is the one who thinks of himself least. No one leads such a bad and sinful life as the one who looks only to his own interests. Indeed, in order to stress how much we should love our neighbour, the Lord has made self-love the standard, because there is no stronger emotion. The force of the expression ought to be carefully assessed. The Lord does not (as some theologians have stupidly imagined) give first place to self-love and the

second to love of others. Rather, he transfers to others the love we naturally feel for ourselves. So the apostle maintains that love 'is not self-seeking' (1 Cor. 13:5). The argument that the thing regulated must always be inferior to the rule is futile. The Lord did not make self-love the rule, as if love to others was inferior to it. Because through natural frailty the feeling of love is usually directed to ourselves, he shows that it ought to spread in another direction; we should be ready to do good to our neighbour with no less eagerness, warmth and concern than for ourselves.

55. Because our Saviour has shown in the parable of the good Samaritan (Luke 10:36) that the term 'neighbour' includes the most distant stranger, there is no excuse for limiting the maxim of love to our own circle. Of course, the closer the relation, the more frequent our acts of kindness should be. Our human situation leads to more ties in common between those who are linked by relationship, friendship or neighbourhood. This is acceptable to God; indeed, his plan for mankind makes it inevitable. Nevertheless, we must embrace the whole human race in our charitable feelings. There can be no distinction between Greek and barbarian, worthy and unworthy, friend and foe, since they must all be seen, not in themselves, but in God. If we reject this idea, it is no wonder we get caught in error. If we want to get on the right track in loving, we must look first to God, not to man: that more often produces hate than love! God demands that the love we bear to him should be spread abroad among all mankind. Our basic principle must always be that, whatever a person may be like, we must still love him, because we love God.
[56–59]

Chapter 9

Christ, although known to the Jews under the Law, was clearly made known only through the Gospel.

[1–3]

4. We can see the error of those who compare the Law with the Gospel, representing it simply as a comparison between the merit of works and the unearned status of righteousness. The contrast between Law and Gospel is not to be thrown out completely, because by the term Law, Paul frequently implies the demand for holy living which God has every right to make. He gives no hope of eternal life unless we obey fully, and pronounces judgment for the slightest failure. Paul shows that we are freely accepted by God and accounted righteous only when we are forgiven, because such obedience to the Law for which a reward is promised could never be found. So he rightly represents the righteousness of the Law and the Gospel as diametrically opposed. But the Gospel has not succeeded the Law in such a way as to usher in a different plan of salvation. On the contrary, it confirms the Law and proves that everything it promised is fulfilled. What was shadow, it has made substance. When Christ says that the Law and the Prophets were in existence until John appeared, he does not relegate the fathers to the judgment which, as slaves of the Law, they would not be able to escape. He suggests that they only possessed basic truth and were inferior to the height of Gospel doctrine.

So Paul, after calling the Gospel 'the power of God for the salvation of everyone who believes', shortly afterwards adds 'to which the Law and the Prophets testify' (Rom. 1:16; 3:21). At the end of the same epistle, though he describes 'the proclamation of Jesus Christ' as 'the revelation of the mystery hidden for long ages past', he modifies the expression by adding that it is 'now revealed ... through the prophetic writings' (Rom. 16:25, 26). So we infer that when the whole Law is referred to, the Gospel differs from it only by clarity of expression. However, because of the unsearchable riches of grace set before us in Christ, there is every reason for saying that by his coming the kingdom of heaven was erected on earth.

[5]
[Chapters 10–11]

Part VII

THE PERSON OF JESUS CHRIST AND HIS WORK OF REDEMPTION

Chapter 12

Christ had to become man to perform the office of Mediator.

[1]

2. Christ's work as Mediator was unique: it was to restore us to divine favour and to make us sons of God, instead of sons of men; heirs of a heavenly kingdom instead of heirs of hell. Only the Son of God could do this by becoming the Son of man. He so received what is ours as to transfer to us what is his. What is his by nature can become ours by grace. Relying on this pledge, we trust that we are the sons of God, because the Son of God took upon himself a body like our body, flesh of our flesh, bone of our bone, that he might be one with us. He did not refuse to take what was distinctive to us, so that he in turn could give us what was distinctive to him. Thus he became both Son of God and Son of man, like us. He himself calls us his brothers when he says, 'I am returning to my Father and your Father, to my God and your God' (John 20:17). In this way we can be sure of our inheritance in the heavenly kingdom, because the only Son of God, to whom it all belongs, has adopted us as brothers. If we are brothers, we are partners with him in his inheritance (Rom. 8:17). It was therefore essential that the one who was to be our redeemer should be truly God and truly man. He was to swallow up death, and only life could do that. He was to conquer sin, and only righteousness could do that. He was to scatter the powers of the air and earth and only a mighty power, superior to both, could do that. But God alone possesses life and righteousness, and the total rule of

heaven. So God, in his infinite mercy, having resolved to redeem us, became our redeemer himself, in the person of his only begotten Son.

3. Another vital factor in our reconciliation with God was that man, who had lost himself by his disobedience, had to substitute obedience as a solution, to satisfy God's justice and pay the penalty of sin. So our Lord came as truly man, adopted the nature of Adam and took his name, so that he might, in his place, obey the Father; and so that he might offer our flesh as the price of satisfying the just judgment of God, and in the same flesh pay the penalty we had incurred. Finally, since as God alone he could not suffer and as man alone he could not conquer death, he combined the human nature with the divine. Then he could subject the weakness of the human to death, for an expiation of sin, and by the power of the divine could achieve for us victory over death. So those who rob Christ of divinity or humanity either detract from his glory or obscure his goodness. They hurt men too, undermining their faith which cannot stand without this foundation ...
[4–7]
[Chapter 13]

Chapter 14

How two natures constitute the one person of the Mediator.

1. When it is said that the Word was made flesh, we must not infer that he was changed into flesh or blended with flesh, but that he chose the Virgin's womb as a temple where he might live. He who was the Son of God, became the Son of man, not by blending the substances but by being one person. We believe that the divine nature was united with the human in such a way that the characteristics of

each remain complete, and yet the two together make up only one Christ. The closest analogy in human affairs to this mystery is of man who is both soul and body. They are not blended together but keep their own separate characteristics. Things can be said of the soul which do not apply to the body and vice versa. Things can be said of the whole man which do not apply either to soul or body separately. Finally, attributes of the soul are transferred to the body, and attributes of the body to the soul, and yet these form only one man. Such means of expression indicate that there is one person made up of two parts, and that these two different natures make one person. The Scriptures speak similarly of Christ. At times they attribute to him qualities which refer particularly to his humanity or divinity, and sometimes those which embrace both natures. The unity of Christ's two natures is expressed so carefully that the Scriptures sometimes apply to one nature the qualities of the other, a figure of speech which the early fathers called 'a communication of properties'.

[2–8]

Chapter 15

Three things to be chiefly regarded in Christ – his offices of prophet, king and priest.

1. Though unbelievers assert the name of Christ, Augustine rightly states that they have no common ground with the godly. Christ belongs exclusively to the Church. If the things which belong to Christ are carefully thought about, it is obvious that he can be with those outside the Church only in name and not reality ... So that faith may find in Christ a sure foundation for salvation, and so rest in him, we must start out with the fact that the function he received from the Father was threefold. He was appointed prophet, king and priest...

Chapter 16

How Christ performed the office of redeemer in procuring our salvation. His death, resurrection and ascension into heaven.

1. All that we have said of Christ up to now leads to this one conclusion: that condemned, dead and lost as we are in ourselves, we must seek righteousness, deliverance, life and salvation in him. So Peter reminds us in the familiar words 'Salvation is found in no-one else, for there is no other name under heaven given to men by which we must be saved' (Acts 4:12). The name of Jesus was not given to him by chance or by the will of man, but was brought from heaven by an angel, heralding God's decree. The reason was given too: 'because he will save his people from their sins' (Matt. 1:21; Luke 1:31). So the work of redeemer was given to him in order that he might be our Saviour. Redemption would be incomplete if it did not lead us to the final goal of safety. The moment we turn aside from Christ in the slightest degree, salvation which rests entirely in him gradually disappears. So all who do not rest in him voluntarily deprive themselves of grace. Bernard's observation deserves to be noted: 'The name of Jesus is not only light but food. It is oil without which food for the soul is dry and salt without which it is insipid. It is honey in the mouth, melody in the ear and joy in the heart. It has healing power. Every discussion where his name is not heard is pointless.'

Here we must think carefully how we obtain salvation from him, so that we shall be convinced that he is its Author. Then, having accepted all that is necessary for a sure foundation of our faith, we may avoid all that might make us doubt. No one can look in on himself and seriously assess his life, without feeling that God is angry and at enmity with him. So he longs anxiously to find a way of regaining his favour. The assurance needed is considerable: until sinners are released from guilt, they are under God's wrath. Because he is a just Judge, he cannot allow his Law to be broken with impunity and demands vengeance.

2. Before we go any further, we must try to see how God, who goes before us in mercy, was our enemy until he was reconciled to us by Christ. But how could he have given us that unique seal of his love – the gift of his only begotten Son – if he had not already freely embraced us in his favour?

As this seems to be a contradiction, I shall try to explain. The way in which the Spirit usually speaks in Scripture is that God was the enemy of men until they were restored to favour by the death of Christ (Rom. 5:10). They were under a curse until their sin was expiated by the sacrifice of Christ (Gal. 3:10, 13). They were separated from God, until they were reunited in Christ's body (Col. 1:21, 22). These expressions help us to understand how wretched our state is without Christ. If it was not stated clearly that divine wrath and vengeance and eternal death hang over us, we would be less aware of our condemnation without the mercy of God, and less likely to value the blessings of salvation. For instance, if a person is told that God could have hated him as a sinner and rejected him with destruction as the deserved punishment, but instead he freely kept him in his favour, that person will be deeply affected and made aware how much he owes to God's mercy. Even more, let him be told, as Scripture teaches, that he was estranged from God by sin, an heir of wrath and sentenced to eternal death. He was cut off from all hope of salvation, an alien from the blessing of God, the slave of Satan and under the yoke of sin. In short, he was doomed to a terrible destruction and already involved in it. Then Christ stepped in, took the punishment upon himself and bore the judgment due to sinners. With his own blood he expiated the sins which made them enemies of God and thereby satisfied him. By his intercessions, he appeased God's anger, and on this

basis created peace between God and men, and by this bond secured God's goodwill towards them. As he thinks of all this, of the disaster he had escaped, wouldn't anyone be deeply moved? To sum up, our minds cannot lay hold of life with sufficient eagerness, or accept it with suitable gratitude, unless we have first been made afraid of divine anger and the thought of eternal death. So we are instructed by divine truth to understand that without Christ, God is in some way hostile to us and has to lift his arm to destroy. Then we look to Christ alone for divine favour and fatherly love!
[3–4]

5. If you ask me how Christ, by abolishing sin, removed the enmity between God and us and purchased the righteousness which makes him kindly disposed to us, the simple answer is that he accomplished it by his total obedience. Paul's testimony bears this out: 'For just as through the disobedience of the one man the many were made sinners, so also through the obedience of the one man the many will be made righteous' (Rom. 5:19). Again he attributes the ground of our pardon, which frees us from the curse of the Law, to the whole life of Christ: 'But when the time had fully come, God sent his Son, born of a woman, born under law, to redeem those under law' (Gal. 4:4–5). So even at his baptism he declared that a part of righteousness was fulfilled by his yielding obedience to the Father's command (Matt. 3:15). In fact, from the moment he took the form of a servant, he began to pay the price of deliverance in order to redeem us. However, in order to define the way of salvation more clearly, Scripture ascribes it especially to the death of Christ. He himself declares that he gave his life as a ransom for many (Matt. 20:28). Paul teaches that he died for our sins (Rom. 4:25). John the Baptist exclaimed 'Look, the Lamb of God, who takes away the sin of the world!' (John 1:29) ... In order to remove our condemnation it was not enough for him to endure just any kind of

death. To obtain our ransom, it was essential to choose a type of death in which he could deliver us, both by giving himself up to condemnation and also undertaking our expiation. If he had been mown down by assassins or killed in a rebellion, there could have been no satisfaction. But when he stands as a criminal at the bar and witnesses are brought to give evidence against him and the judge condemns him to death, we see him taking on the character of an offender. Here we must refer to two things which had been foretold by the prophets, and serve admirably to confirm our faith. When we read that Christ was led away from the judgment seat to execution, and was crucified between thieves, we have a fulfilment of the prophecy '[he] was numbered with the transgressors' (Isa. 53:12; Mark 15:20, 27). Why did it have to be? So that he might bear the character of a sinner, not of a just or innocent person, in that he died on account of sin. On the other hand, we read that he was acquitted by the same lips that condemned him, because Pilate was forced to bear public testimony to his innocence. This reminds us of the Psalmist: 'I am forced to restore what I did not steal' (Ps. 69:4). So we see Christ taking on the character of a sinner and a criminal, while at the same time his innocence shines out, and it becomes obvious that he is suffering for another's crime and not his own. He suffered under Pontius Pilate, being ranked among criminals by the formal sentence of the judge, and yet he is declared innocent by the same judge, when he affirms that he can find no cause of death in him (John 18:38). Our acquittal lies in this: that the guilt which made us liable to punishment was transferred to the head of the Son of God. It is really important to remember that he has taken our place, so that we may not spend all our lives in trepidation and anxiety, as if the punishment we deserve, but which the Son of God took to himself, was still hanging over us.

6. The very nature of his death contains a striking truth. The cross was cursed, not only in the opinion of men, but by

the carrying out of divine Law. So Christ, while hanging on it, subjected himself to the curse. This had to be done so that the whole curse, which we deserved because of sin, might be taken from us by being transferred to him ... The apostle states this even more plainly when he says that 'God made him who had no sin to be sin for us, so that in him we might become the righteousness of God' (2 Cor. 5:21). The Son of God, though spotlessly pure, took upon himself the disgrace and shame of our iniquity, and in return clothed us with his purity. He seems to refer to the same thing when he says that God 'condemned sin in sinful man' (Rom. 8:3) having destroyed the power of sin when it was transferred to the body of Christ. The verse indicates that Christ, in his death, was offered to the Father as a propitiatory victim and that because expiation was made by his sacrifice, we can stop trembling at divine wrath. It is now clear what the prophet means when he says 'the Lord has laid on him the iniquity of us all' (Isa. 53:6). As he was to wash away the filth of sin, it was transferred to him by imputation. The cross to which he was nailed was a symbol of this, as the apostle proclaims 'Christ redeemed us from the curse of the law by becoming a curse for us, for it is written: "Cursed is everyone who is hung on a tree." He redeemed us in order that the blessing given to Abraham might come to the Gentiles through Christ Jesus' (Gal. 3:13–14). In the same way Peter says that he 'bore our sins in his body on the tree' (1 Pet. 2:24). From the very symbol of the cross, we see more clearly that the burden with which we were oppressed was laid upon him. We must not think that he was overwhelmed by the curse which he endured, but rather that by enduring it, he held down, broke and finally wiped out all its power. So faith lays hold of acquittal in Christ's condemnation, and blessing in his curse. Hence it is with good reason that Paul triumphantly celebrates the victory which Christ obtained upon the cross, as if the cross, that symbol of ignominy, had been transformed into a triumphal chariot! He reminds us that he blotted out the handwriting or ordinance that was

against us, and took it out of the way, nailing it to his cross:
'And having disarmed the powers and authorities, he made
a public spectacle of them, triumphing over them by the
cross' (Col. 2:14–15). Another apostle declares that Christ
'through the eternal Spirit offered himself unblemished to
God' (Heb. 9:14). Hence that transformation of the cross,
which would otherwise be impossible. In order for these
things to take deep root in our inmost hearts, we must never
lose sight of sacrifice and purification. If Christ had not
been a victim, we could have no certainty of his being our
substitute, ransom and propitiation. So blood is always
mentioned whenever Scripture explains the way of salvation. The shedding of Christ's blood was not only for propitiation but for the cleansing of sin.

7. The Creed mentions next that he 'was dead and buried'.
Here again we must think how he took our place in order to
pay the price of our redemption. We were under the yoke
of death, but he put himself in its power in our place, so that
he might free us from it. This is what the apostle meant
when he says 'so that ... he might taste death for everyone'
(Heb. 2:9). By dying he prevented us from dying. By his
death he purchased life for us. But in allowing himself to be
overcome by death, it was not to be swallowed up in its
abyss but rather to annihilate it so that it could not annihilate us. He did not allow himself to be subdued by it, so as
to be crushed by its power. Rather he laid it low, when it
was hanging over us and crowing as though we were already
defeated. In short, his purpose was 'that by his death he
might destroy him who holds the power of death – that is,
the devil – and free those who all their lives were held in
slavery by their fear of death' (Heb. 2:14–15). This was the
firstfruit of his death for us. Another is that by fellowship
with him he crushes our earthly parts so that they will not be
active any more, and kills the old man so that he will not
flourish and bring forth fruit. The effect of Christ's burial is
that we, as his followers, are buried to sin. The apostle says

that we are grafted into the likeness of Christ's death (Rom. 6:5), and that we are buried to sin with him, so that the world is crucified to us by his cross and we to the world (Gal. 2:19; 6:14). We are dead with Christ (Col. 3:3), so Paul not only urges us to present ourselves an example of his death, but affirms that there is an efficacy in it which should be apparent in all Christians, if only they would not make his death pointless. So in the death and burial of Christ, there is a double blessing. There is rescue from death to which we were in bondage, and the putting to death of our flesh.
[8–9]

10. How should we understand Christ's 'descent into hell' which is mentioned in the Creed? The Word of God explains it in a way which is inspired and full of marvellous comfort. Nothing would have been achieved if Christ had only suffered physical death. In order to come between us and God's anger, to satisfy his righteous judgment, it was necessary for him to feel the full force of divine vengeance. It was also necessary for him to engage at close quarters with the powers of hell and the horror of eternal death. Isaiah said that 'the chastisement of our peace was upon him,' that he 'was bruised for our iniquities,' that he had 'borne our infirmities' (Isa. 53:4, 5 AV). These expressions show that, like a sponsor for those guilty and condemned, he paid all the penalties which we owed. The one exception was that death could not hold him (Acts 2:24). So there is nothing odd in saying that he descended into hell, seeing he endured the death which God has to inflict on the sinner. It is ridiculous to object that this makes a mockery of the order of the Creed, because an event which came before burial is placed after it. After explaining what Christ endured, the Creed rightly speaks of the unseen and incomprehensible judgment which he endured from God. This teaches us that not only was Christ's body given as the price of our redemption, but there was a greater and even more

amazing price: he bore in his soul the torture due to condemned and ruined man.
[11–12]

13. Now comes the resurrection from the dead, without which everything else would be incomplete. Because the cross, death and burial of Christ speak of weakness, faith must go beyond them all in order to become strong. So although we have complete salvation through his death, because we are reconciled to God by it, it is by his resurrection, not his death, that we are said to be born again to a living hope (1 Pet. 1:3). As he became victorious over death by rising again, so the victory of our faith is because of his resurrection. This is well expressed by Paul: 'He was delivered over to death for our sins and was raised to life for our justification' (Rom. 4:25). In other words, by his death sin was taken away and by his resurrection righteousness was restored. How could he have freed us from death by dying, if he had yielded to its power? How could he have gained the victory for us, if he had fallen in the fight? Our salvation is thus divided between the death and resurrection of Christ. Sin and death were wiped out by the former and righteousness and life were restored by the latter. We must remember that when in Scripture Christ's death alone is mentioned, everything to do with the resurrection is included. In the same way, when the resurrection alone is mentioned, everything to do with Christ's death is included. As he obtained the victory by rising again and became the resurrection and the life, Paul rightly argues: 'And if Christ has not been raised, your faith is futile; you are still in your sins' (1 Cor. 15:17). Again, in another passage, after exulting in the death of Christ as against the fear of condemnation he speaks of 'Christ Jesus, who died – more than that, who was raised to life – is at the right hand of God and is also interceding for us' (Rom. 8:34). The putting to death of our flesh depends on the link with his cross

and resurrection. As the apostle says, 'just as Christ was raised from the dead through the glory of the Father, we too may live a new life' (Rom. 6:4). In another verse he teaches that, being dead with Christ, we must 'Put to death, therefore, whatever belongs to your earthly nature' (Col. 3:5). As we are risen with Christ he tells us to 'set your hearts on things above, where Christ is seated at the right hand of God' (Col. 3:1). In these words we are not only encouraged by the example of our risen Saviour to follow newness of life, but are taught that by his power we are restored to righteousness. A third benefit we derive is that, like a pledge, his resurrection assures us of our own. This subject is discussed at length in 1 Corinthians 15:12–26, but we can observe in passing that when he is said to have 'risen from the dead', the phrase expresses the reality both of his death and resurrection. He died the same death as other men naturally die, and received immortality in the same mortal flesh he had taken on.

14. The resurrection is naturally followed by the ascension into heaven. By rising again Christ began to display his glory and goodness fully, having put behind him his lowly human life and the shame of the cross. But it was only by his ascension to heaven that his reign really began. The apostle bears this out when he says he ascended 'in order to fill the whole universe' (Eph. 4:10). This reminds us that although he left us, it was so that he might mean even more to us than when his presence was confined to a human body here on earth. So John, after repeating the famous invitation 'If anyone is thirsty, let him come to me and drink' immediately adds 'Up to that time the Spirit had not been given' (John 7:37, 39). The Lord also told his disciples 'It is for your good that I am going away. Unless I go away, the Counsellor will not come to you' (John 16:7). To comfort them for his bodily absence, he tells them he will not leave them comfortless, but will come again. This time his coming would be invisible but even more precious. They would

know that his reign and power would enable them, as faithful followers, not only to live well but also to die happily. That's exactly what happened! His Spirit was poured out abundantly, his kingdom was advanced gloriously and a much greater power was available to strengthen his followers and upset his enemies. When he returned to heaven, he withdrew his physical presence from our sight. He didn't stop being with the disciples but by the ascension fulfilled his promise to be with us to the end of the world. As his body was raised to heaven, so his power and reign have spread to the uttermost parts.

15. Now comes the phrase that he 'sat at the right hand of God'. The metaphor comes from princes who have judges to whom they delegate the job of administration and issuing commands. So Christ, in whom the Father is pleased to reign, is said to have been received up and seated on his right hand (Mark 16:19). It is as if he was put in control of heaven and earth and formally admitted to a position of administration until the day of judgment. The apostle implies this when he says that the Father 'seated him at his right hand in the heavenly realms, far above all rule and authority, power and dominion, and every title that can be given, not only in the present age but also in the one to come. And God placed all things under his feet and appointed him to be head over everything for the church' (Eph. 1:20–2; 1 Cor. 15:27). You can see now why he is seated there: so that every creature in heaven and earth should reverence his majesty, do him homage and submit to his power. All that the apostles mean when they refer to Christ's seat at the Father's right hand, is that everything is at his disposal (Acts 2:30–6; 3:21; Heb. 1:8). It is an error to think that it only indicates a blessed state. In Acts 7:56 we read that Stephen saw him standing. This does not refer to the position of his body but the majesty of his kingdom. Sitting simply means presiding on the judgment seat of heaven.

16. Faith derives several advantages from this doctrine. First, it grasps that the Lord, by his ascension, has opened up the way to heaven, which Adam had shut. As he has entered it in our flesh, it follows that in a way we are ourselves seated in heavenly places (Eph. 2:5f.); not merely hoping for heaven but possessing it in our minds. Second, faith can grasp that his seat beside the Father is of real advantage to us. Having entered the temple not made with hands, he constantly appears as our advocate and intercessor in the Father's presence (Heb. 7:25; 9:11–12; Rom. 8:34). He directs attention to his own righteousness and turns it away from our sins. He reconciles us to God; by his intercession he paves the way of access to the throne of grace for us sinners. Third, faith can see Christ's power, on which our strength, resources and triumph over hell depend. 'When he ascended on high, he led captives in his train and gave gifts to men' (Eph. 4:8). He defeated his foes, gave gifts to his people and showered them with spiritual riches. So he occupies his seat on high, transferring his virtue to us and quickening us to spiritual life. He sanctifies us by his Spirit and adorns his Church with various graces, preserving it from all harm. By the strength of his hand he holds back the enemies which rage against his cross and our salvation. He does all this so that he may possess all power in heaven and earth, until he has completely vanquished all his foes and ours, and completed the building of his Church (Ps. 110:1). This is the real nature of the kingdom and this is the power which the Father has given him, until he completes his last act by judging the quick and the dead.

17. Christ gives his followers certain proof of his present power, but because his kingdom in the world is obscured in some ways by its humble earthly condition it is best for faith to dwell on his visible presence at the last day. He will descend from heaven in visible form, just as he was seen to ascend (Acts 1:11; Matt. 24:30). He will appear to everyone with the inexpressible majesty of his kingdom, the glory of

immortality and the limitless power of the Godhead and surrounded by a host of angels. So we are told to wait for our redeemer until that day when he will separate the sheep from the goats and the elect from the reprobate (Matt. 25:31–3). Not one person, living or dead, will escape his judgment. The sound of a trumpet summoning the quick and the dead to his tribunal will be heard to the ends of the earth (1 Thess. 4:16–17) ...

18. What a comfort it is to think that judgment rests with the one who has planned that we should share the honour with him (Matt. 19:28)! This proves that in no way will he ascend the judgment seat to condemn us. How could a compassionate prince destroy his own people? How could a head scatter the other parts of the body? How could an advocate condemn his clients? If the apostle, referring to Christ's mediation, can exclaim boldly 'Who is he that condemns?' (Rom. 8:34), how much more definite it is that Christ the intercessor, will not condemn those under his protection. What security it gives, to know that we shall not be judged at any other tribunal than that of our redeemer to whom we look for salvation! The one who promises eternal bliss in the Gospel will one day, as Judge, confirm that promise. The Father honoured the Son by committing all judgment to him (John 5:22) so that he could quieten the consciences of his people, when they were terrified at the thought of judgment.

I have followed the sequence of the Apostles' Creed until now, because it has the most important statements about redemption in a few words, yet separately and distinctly ...

19. When we see that the whole sum of our salvation, and every little bit of it, are wrapped up in Christ (Acts 4:12), we must beware of trying to get the minutest particle from any other source. If we look for salvation, the very name of Jesus teaches us that it is in him (1 Cor. 1:30). If we look for any other gifts of the Spirit, we shall find them in his anoint-

ing. We shall also find strength in his reign, purity in his conception, and kindness in his nativity, when he was made like us in every way so that he might sympathise with us (Heb. 2:17). If we seek for redemption, we shall find it in his passion; acquittal, in his condemnation; remission of the curse, in his cross (Gal. 3:13); satisfaction, in his sacrifice; purification, in his blood; reconciliation, in his descent to hell; mortification of the flesh, in his sepulchre; newness of life in his resurrection, and immortality too; the inheritance of a celestial kingdom, in his entrance into heaven; protection, security and the abundant supply of every blessing, in his kingdom; secure anticipation of judgment in his power to judge. In conclusion, since every kind of blessing is treasured up in him, we must draw our whole supply from him and none from anywhere else. Those who are not satisfied with him alone and entertain various hopes from others (though they still look mainly to him) veer from the right path simply because their thoughts are elsewhere. This can never happen if we really know the abundance of his blessings!

[Chapter 17]

Part VIII

FAITH AND REPENTANCE

BOOK THREE

THE WAY OF OBTAINING THE GRACE OF CHRIST. ITS BENEFITS, ITS EFFECTS.

Chapter 1

Christ's benefits profit us through the secret work of the Spirit.

1. Now we must look at the way we can obtain the blessings which God has bestowed in Christ, not for private use, but to help the poor and needy. The first thing we have to realise is that, as long as we are without Christ, nothing which he did to achieve salvation is of any use to us. In order to pass on to us the blessings which he received from the Father, he must become ours and live in us. He is called our head (Eph. 4:15) and the first-born among many brethren (Rom. 8:29), so we are grafted into him (Rom. 11:17) and clothed with him (Gal. 3:27). Until we become one with him, everything he possesses is nothing to us. This is gained by faith, but not everyone lays hold of Christ's offer made in the Gospel. So we have to look further and find out about the secret working of the Spirit, and how it is, through him that we enjoy Christ and all his blessings ... The Holy Spirit is the bond by which Christ effectively binds us to himself.
[2]

3. ... Until we concentrate our minds on the Spirit, Christ does nothing for us, because we view him detachedly and at a distance. He benefits only those to whom he is a head (Eph. 4:15) and the first-born among the brethren (Rom. 8:29); to those who are clothed with him. Only then is his coming not in vain. It is a sacred marriage, by which we become bone of his bone and flesh of his flesh, and so one with him (Eph. 5:30). It is by the Spirit alone that he unites himself to us. By the grace and energy of the Spirit we become his members, so that he is in charge of us and we, in our turn, possess him.
[4]

Chapter 2

Faith. Its definition and characteristics.

[1–5]

6. The true knowledge of Christ consists in receiving him as he is offered by the Father; that is, empowered with the Gospel. He is the object of our faith and we cannot find the way to him without the guidance of the Gospel. There we find the treasures of grace unfolded to us. If it remained closed, Christ would mean little to us. So Paul makes faith and doctrine inseparable in those words 'You, however, did not come to know Christ that way. Surely you heard of him and were taught in him in accordance with the truth that is in Jesus' (Eph. 4:20–1). Enough was revealed to Moses and the prophets to form a foundation for faith, but the Gospel manifests Christ more fully. Paul rightly calls it the doctrine of faith (1 Tim. 4:6) ...

We must remember that there is an inseparable link between faith and the Word, and that they can no more be separated than rays of light from the sun ... So if faith goes off course by the least degree from the mark at which it

ought to aim, it is no longer faith but becomes wavering
doubt and uncertain mind. The Word is the base on which
faith rests and is strengthened. If it moves from it, it falls.
Take away the Word, and there will be no faith. We are not
discussing here whether the ministry of man is necessary to
spread the Word of God by which faith is born, but we are
saying that the Word itself, however it comes to us, is like
a mirror in which faith can see God. Whether he uses man
as his agent or works directly by his own power, it is always
by his Word that he manifests himself to those he plans to
draw to himself. So Paul describes faith as the obedience
given to the Gospel (Rom. 1:5) and writing to the Philippians, he commends them for the obedience of faith (Phil.
2:17).

Faith includes not merely the knowledge that God exists,
but especially a realisation of his will towards us. We need
to know not only what he is in himself, but also the character he chooses to reveal to us. Faith is the knowledge of the
divine will towards us, discovered from his Word. Its pre-
requisite is a conviction of the truth of God. So long as your
mind entertains any doubts as to the truth of the Word, its
authority will be weak and doubtful. Or rather, it will have
no authority at all. It is not enough to believe that God is
true and cannot lie or deceive, unless you feel firmly convinced that every word which proceeds from him is sacred,
absolute truth.

7. Since men's hearts are not moved to faith by every Word
of God, we must consider what does cause them to respond. God's declaration to Adam was 'you will surely die'
(Gen. 2:17) and to Cain 'Your brother's blood cries out to
me from the ground' (Gen. 4:10), but these, far from establishing faith, would seem to shake it. We do not deny that
it is in the nature of faith to assent to God's truth in whatever way he speaks: we only want to find out what faith can
find in God's Word, to lean and to rely upon. When conscience is only aware of wrath and indignation, how can it do

anything but tremble and be afraid and how can it avoid turning away from the God whom it dreads? But faith ought to seek God, not turn away from him. It is obvious, therefore, that we have not yet found a complete definition of faith, because it is impossible to name every sort of knowledge of the divine will. So for 'will', often the messenger of bad news and the herald of fear, let us substitute the kindness or mercy of God. In this way we shall undoubtedly be coming nearer to the nature of faith.

We are drawn to seek God when we are told that our safety is treasured up in him; we are confirmed in this when he declares that he takes a deep interest in our welfare. We need his gracious promise that he is a propitious Father, since there is no other way in which we can approach him. So mercy and truth are closely linked in the Psalms. It would be useless to know that God is true, if he did not lovingly draw us to himself. We could not lay hold of his mercy, if he did not offer it.

> I speak of your faithfulness and salvation. I do not conceal your love and your truth from the great assembly. Do not withhold your mercy from me, O Lord; may your love and your truth always protect me (Ps. 40:10–11).

… It would be presumptuous to believe that God was well-disposed towards us, if we did not have his assurance and clear invitation. Christ is the only pledge of love, for without him, everything speaks of hatred and anger.

Since the knowledge of divine goodness cannot be of much importance unless it leads us to trust in it, we must not allow knowledge to be mingled with doubt. But the human mind, when blind and dark, is unable to rise to a true knowledge of the divine will. Nor can the heart, vacillating in constant doubt, rest secure in such knowledge. So, in order that the Word of God may be given full credit, the mind must be enlightened and the heart strengthened from some other direction. We shall have a complete definition of faith

if we say that it is a firm and sure knowledge of God's favour towards us, based on the truth of a free promise in Christ, revealed to our minds and sealed on our hearts by the Holy Spirit.
[8–13]

14. Now I want to go over the different parts of our definition one by one, so that no doubts can remain. By knowledge, we do not mean the sort of understanding we have through our human senses. This knowledge is far superior: the human mind has to go out of and beyond itself to reach it. Even when it has reached it, it does not comprehend what it feels, but understands more from persuasion than it could discern by its own ability... Paul says that 'as long as we are at home in the body we are away from the Lord. We live by faith, not by sight' (2 Cor. 5:6–7) showing that what we understand by faith is distant from us and out of view. So we conclude that the knowledge of faith consists more in certainty than discernment.

15. We must add that faith is sure and certain, so that we can convey an impression of its strength and unchanging nature. As faith is not happy with a doubting, changing mind, so it cannot be happy with obscure and vague ideas. It calls for a certainty which is complete and decisive, only to be expected in matters which are sure and proven. Unbelief is so deeply rooted in our hearts that while everyone confesses with their lips that God is faithful, no one ever believes it without a tremendous struggle. Particularly when we are brought to the test, we betray our unbelief by wavering. With good reason, the Holy Spirit bears clear testimony to the authority of God, so that it may deal with this problem and make us really believe the divine promises: 'And the words of the Lord are flawless, like silver refined in a furnace of clay, purified seven times' (Ps. 12:6) ...
Whenever God commends his Word, he is indirectly re-

buking our unbelief, because he says it to remove all false
doubts from our hearts. So many people have a picture of
divine mercy which gives them very little comfort. They are
haunted by terrible anxiety as they doubt whether God will
forgive them. They imagine that they have grasped the
truth about his mercy, but they put such narrow limitations
on it. They have the idea that this mercy is great and over-
flowing. They believe it has been given to many and is available to all. But they cannot be sure whether it will reach
them personally, or rather, whether they can reach it. So
their knowledge stops short and leaves them in mid-air. Far
from being strong and peaceful in mind, they are weighed
down with doubt and apprehension. How different is the
feeling of full assurance which the Scriptures attach to faith
– an assurance which leaves us in no doubt that God's goodness is clearly offered to us. We cannot have this assurance
without being aware of its sweetness, and experiencing it in
our hearts. So the apostle deduces that confidence follows
faith, and boldness follows confidence. His words are 'In
him and through faith in him we may approach God with
freedom and confidence' (Eph. 3:12). This underlines the
fact that our faith is not real unless it enables us to stand
calmly in the presence of God. Such boldness can only
spring from confidence in God's favour and salvation. This
is so true that the term faith is often used as a synonym for
confidence.

16. The main hinge on which faith turns is this: we must not
imagine that the Lord's promises are true objectively but
not in our experience. We must make them ours by embracing them in our hearts. Only then will confidence (referred
to as peace in Romans 5:1) spring to life. This is the assurance which quietens and soothes the conscience before
God's judgment. Without it, it is plagued and torn apart
with overwhelming fear (unless it takes a momentary nap,
forgetting God and itself). And it really is momentary! It
can never enjoy oblivion for long, because the memory of

God's judgment constantly recurs and cuts to the quick. A true believer is one who is firmly convinced that he is reconciled to God, his loving heavenly Father. He looks to him for everything and trusts his promises, claiming salvation with unwavering confidence. The apostle comments: 'We have come to share in Christ if we hold firmly till the end the confidence we had at first' (Heb. 3:14). In other words, you can't have strong faith in the Lord unless you are gloriously confident of being an heir to the heavenly kingdom. No man is a believer unless, sure in the certainty of his salvation, he triumphs bravely over the devil and death. So Paul exclaims:

> For I am convinced that neither death nor life, neither angels nor demons, neither the present nor the future, nor any powers, neither height nor depth, nor anything else in all creation, will be able to separate us from the love of God that is in Christ Jesus our Lord (Rom. 8:38–39).

In the same way, Paul does not think that the eyes of our understanding are open, unless we know the hope of the eternal inheritance to which we are called (Eph. 1:18). He consistently suggests throughout his letters that God's goodness is not really understood when the fruit of assurance does not result.

17. I am sure some will say that this is very different from the experience of many believers. They recognise God's grace towards them, but often feel anxious and sometimes even tremble with fear, so strong are the temptations which attack the mind. This hardly seems consistent with the certainty of faith, and we must try to resolve the dilemma. When we say that faith must be certain and secure, we don't mean that assurance is never touched by doubt or anxiety. Indeed, we know that believers have a constant struggle with doubt, and are very aware that con-

science does not always enjoy peace and quiet, unaffected by turmoil. On the other hand, whatever the means of attack, there is no excuse for falling away from faith and throwing up the sure hope which in God's mercy they have received. Scripture does not give us a better example of faith than David, especially if we look at the consistency of his life. But it is obvious from his writings that his mind was often far from being at peace. When he rebukes his turbulent soul, he is condemning himself for unbelief: 'Why are you downcast, O my soul? Why so disturbed within me? Put your hope in God' (Ps. 42:5). His fear was a sign of distrust, as if he thought that the Lord had left him. Again he confesses: 'In my alarm I said, "I am cut off from your sight!"' (Ps. 31:22) …

18. To make all this clearer, we must go back to the distinction between flesh and spirit, to which we have already referred, and which is specially relevant here. The believer finds two principles within: the one fills him with delight as he recognises God's goodness; the other fills him with grief as he realises his fallen state. The one leads him to rest on the promise of the Gospel; the other alarms him, convicting him of sin. The one makes him rejoice with the hope of eternal life; the other makes him tremble with the fear of death. This contradiction is because of an imperfect faith, since we will never in this life be completely free of distrust and totally filled with faith. So these conflicts result. Natural doubts attack spiritual faith. But if certainty is mingled with doubt in the believer's mind, do we have to conclude that faith is not sure and clear, but obscure and confused, when it comes to understanding God's will for us? Not at all. Although we are disturbed and confused by distrust, we are not thrown into an abyss. Though we are shaken, we are not driven away. The invariable result is that, in the long run, faith surmounts the difficulties which threaten it.

19. It really all comes to this: when we have an atom of faith in our hearts, we can see God's face, gentle, serene and approving. He is far away of course, but we can discern him clearly enough to know that there is no illusion. As we go on with God (and it ought to be steady progress) we get a closer and clearer view, which becomes more and more familiar as time goes by. A mind illumined with the knowledge of God finds that ignorance gradually disappears. Fortunately incomplete awareness of him does not keep us from a clear grasp of his love for us. This is the most important ingredient of faith. It is like someone shut up in prison, who gets rays of sunshine through a narrow window, though he can't see the sun itself. He has no doubt about the source of light and benefits from it. So believers, hampered by the restrictions of an earthly body and surrounded with much that is obscure, are illumined by any light which reaches them from God. It proves his love and makes them feel safe.
[20–43]

Chapter 3

Regeneration by faith. Repentance.

1. We have been discussing how faith possesses Christ and enables us to enjoy his blessings. The subject would be incomplete if we did not show what can result from this. The message of the Gospel is about repentance and forgiveness of sins. If these are omitted, any discussion about faith will be useless. Since Christ gives us free reconciliation and newness of life (which we grasp by faith) it would be helpful to look at both. The shortest jump is from faith to repentance. If repentance is understood properly, it will be clear that a man is justified freely by faith alone, but true holiness of life is also essential. Repentance not only follows faith but is produced by it. This is indisputable. Pardon and for-

giveness are offered by the preaching of the Gospel, in order that the sinner, freed from Satan's power and the bondage of sin, may move into God's kingdom. But we may be sure that no one can understand the grace of the Gospel without leaving the errors of his old life and taking the right path. His whole aim must be to practise repentance. Those who think that repentance precedes faith, instead of flowing from it or being produced by it (like fruit by the tree), have never understood what it is all about.

2. ... When we attribute the origin of repentance to faith, we are not suggesting that there is a time gap between them. We are merely trying to show that a man cannot honestly say he knows about repentance unless he knows he belongs to God. But no one is really convinced he is of God until he has accepted his offer of love. This will become clearer as we go along. Some people get it wrong, seeing that many submit to God because their consciences are afraid, or are ready to obey him before they know him or anything about his love. This is an initial fear, which some writers commend because they think it is almost as good as true and genuine obedience. But we are not thinking here about the various ways in which Christ draws us to himself, or prepares us to think about piety. I just want to say that no righteousness can be found where the Spirit is not in control. According to the Psalmist, 'with you there is forgiveness; therefore you are feared' (Ps. 130:4). No one will ever honour God if he does not believe that God forgives him. No one will ever willingly obey the Law, if he is not convinced that his efforts are pleasing to God. The goodness of God in bearing with our sins and forgiving them, is a sign of his fatherly love ...
[3–4]

5. ... Paul says in Acts, 'I have declared to both Jews and Greeks that they must turn to God in repentance and have faith in our Lord Jesus' (Acts 20:21). He refers to faith and

repentance as two different things. What do we make of this? Can true repentance exist without faith? No way! But although they cannot be separated, they ought to be distinguished. As there is no faith without hope, and yet faith and hope are different, so repentance and faith, though invariably linked, are not to be confused with one another. I know that the term 'repentance' includes the whole act of turning to God, of which faith is an important part. The term 'repentance' is derived in the Hebrew from conversion or turning again, and in the Greek from a change of mind and purpose. Both definitions are appropriate, because in forsaking ourselves we turn to God, and as we put off the old mind, we put on the new. It seems to me that we could well define repentance like this: it is a true conversion of our life to God, springing from real and solemn fear of God; it consists also in putting to death our flesh, and the quickening of the Spirit ...

6. Now we need to look at three aspects of this definition in particular. First, in the conversion of the life to God we need a transformation of the soul as well as outward things. Only then can old habits be discarded and the fruit of the Spirit be produced. So Ezekiel urges those whom he calls to repentance to get 'a new heart and a new spirit' (Ezek. 18:31) ... No passage teaches us what real repentance is better than Jeremiah 4:1–4: '"If you will return, O Israel, return to me," ... Break up your unploughed ground and do not sow among thorns. Circumcise yourselves to the Lord, circumcise your hearts.' Jeremiah declares that it is useless to begin the study of righteousness unless ungodliness is eradicated from the inmost heart. To stress this further, he reminds the people that they are dealing with God, and can gain nothing by deceit, because he hates a double mind ...

7. The second part of our definition is that repentance springs from a sincere fear of God. Before the sinner's mind turns to repentance, he must be challenged by the thought

of divine judgment. When the thought has gripped his mind that God will one day take the judgment seat to take account of all words and actions, it will not let him have a moment's peace. He will be driven to take on a different life style, so that he will be able to stand confidently at that judgment seat. So the Scriptures, when urging men to repentance, often introduce the subject of judgment as in Jeremiah 'or my wrath will break out and burn like fire because of the evil you have done – burn with no-one to quench it' (Jer. 4:4) … As repentance begins with dread and hatred of sin, the apostle gives godly sorrow as one of its causes (2 Cor. 7:10). By 'godly sorrow' he means that we should not only tremble at the punishment, but hate and detest the sin, because we know it displeases God. Unless we are cut to the quick, the unwillingness of our worldly natures cannot be corrected. Nothing would move us in our indolence unless God lifted his rod and struck deep. There is a rebellious spirit in us which has to be broken by his hammer.

The stern threats which God utters are forced from him by our depraved nature. While we are asleep, it is useless to try and win us by gentle means. The Bible often refers to this. But there is another reason why the fear of God lies at the root of repentance. Even if men were full of every kind of virtue, if they bore no reference to God, however laudable they were in the world, they would be mere abomination in heaven. The most important ingredient of righteousness is to render to God the service and homage due to him. He is shamefully cheated whenever we do not submit to his authority.

8. Now we must explain the third part of the definition, and show what we mean when we say that repentance consists of two parts: the mortification of the flesh, and the quickening of the Spirit. The prophets make this easier for a worldly people by expressing it in simple but clear terms, when they say, 'Turn from evil and do good' (Ps. 34:14).

' … wash and make yourselves clean. Take your evil deeds out of my sight! Stop doing wrong, learn to do right! Seek justice, encourage the oppressed' (Isa. 1:16–17). In dissuading us from evil, they demand the total destruction of the flesh, which is full of falsehood and evil. It is a tremendously hard thing to renounce self and put our own desires on one side. The flesh cannot be considered dead unless everything of ourselves is thrown out. Because all the desires of the flesh are enmity against God (Rom. 8:7), the first step to the obedience of his Law is renouncing our own nature. Renewal becomes evident by the fruits produced, i.e. righteousness, judgment and mercy.

It would not be enough merely to perform such deeds if the mind and heart had not already been filled with the desire for righteousness, judgment and mercy. This happens when the Holy Spirit, instilling holiness within, so inspires our souls with new thoughts and affections that they may be rightly considered new. By nature we are averse to God, and unless self-denial takes over, we shall never lean to what is right. So we are often urged to put off the old man, to renounce the world and the flesh, to forsake our lust, and be renewed in the spirit of our mind. The very term 'putting to death' reminds us how difficult it is to forget our old nature. We cannot learn fear of God and the basic principles of godliness, unless we are pierced by the sword of the Spirit and destroyed. It is as if God were saying that to rank among his sons our ordinary natures must be wiped out.

9. Putting to death of the flesh and quickening of the Spirit both come from our union with Christ. If we have true fellowship in Christ's death, our old man is crucified by his power. The body of sin dies, so that the corruption of our old nature can never really flourish again (Rom. 6:5–6). If we share in his resurrection, we are raised by it to newness of life, which makes us conformed to the righteousness of God.

By the word 'repentance', then, I understand new birth.

Its sole aim is to form in us the image of God which was spoilt and almost destroyed by Adam's sin. The apostle teaches this when he says, 'we, who with unveiled faces all reflect the Lord's glory, are being transformed into his likeness with ever-increasing glory, which comes from the Lord, who is the Spirit' (2 Cor. 3:18). Again, 'to be made new in the attitude of your minds; and to put on the new self, created to be like God in true righteousness and holiness' (Eph. 4:23–24). Again, 'put on the new self, which is being renewed in knowledge in the image of its Creator' (Col. 3:10). So through Christ's blessing we are restored by new birth into the righteousness of God from which we had fallen through Adam. In this way the Lord graciously makes whole all to whom he gives eternal life. This renewal is not achieved in a moment, a day or a year, but by gradual progress God abolishes what is left of carnal sin in his elect. He cleanses them from evil and consecrates them as his temples. He makes them long for true holiness, so that they may practise repentance constantly and know that this spiritual warfare ends only at death ...

10. The children of God are delivered from the bondage of sin by new birth. This does not mean complete freedom and absence of temptation. A ceaseless battle goes on, to exercise the saints and help them to understand their weakness. There is still a spring of evil in every born-again man, which gives rise to sinful desires and actions. Wrong appetites still flourish and, even though resisted, incite us to lust, greed, ambition and other vices ...

11. We read that God purifies his Church, to make it 'holy and blameless' (Eph. 5:26–27), that he promises this cleansing by means of baptism, and that he carries it out in his elect. This obviously refers to guilt rather than sin. In regenerating his people, God accomplishes so much: he destroys the dominion of sin by giving the Spirit to ensure victory in the battle. Sin no longer reigns, but it still remains.

Although we say that the old man is crucified and the law of sin abolished in the children of God (Rom. 6:6), the traces of sin survive, not to have dominion, but to humble us with a realisation of our weakness. We know that these sinful remnants are not held against us and it is just as though they had never been. But we realise that it is only because of God's mercy that the saints are not charged with the guilt which would otherwise make them sinners before him ... [12–25]

Part IX

THE CHRISTIAN LIFE

Chapter 6

The Christian life. How Scripture urges us to it.

[1–3]

4. This is the place to speak to those who want to be called Christians, although they have nothing of Christ's but his name and sign. How dare they claim his sacred name? No one can have fellowship with Christ, unless they have acquired genuine knowledge of him from the Gospel. The apostle denies that anyone has truly learned Christ unless he has learned to put off the 'old self, which is being corrupted by its deceitful desires', and put on Christ (Eph. 4:22). They are guilty of falsely pretending a knowledge of Christ, despite the eloquence with which they talk of the Gospel. Doctrine is not a matter of talk but of life. It is not grasped by intellect alone, like other branches of learning. It is received only when it fills the soul and finds a home in the inmost recesses of the heart. People who boast that they are what they are not, must cease to insult God in this way; or they must show that they are worthy disciples of the divine Master.

We have given doctrine first place because our salvation must start there. But then it must move into the heart and on to our behaviour. Then we shall be transformed and made fruitful. Philosophers are rightly angered when those who profess a skill which ought to rule their lives, merely talk about it, however impressively. We have much more reason to detest these trifling sophists, who are content to talk about the Gospel, when it ought to reach and affect the inner longings of the heart. It should take possession of the soul and influence the whole personality a hundred times more than the sterile discussions of philosophers!

5. I do not insist that the life of the Christian should express nothing but the perfect Gospel, though this would be desirable and should be attempted. I do not insist so firmly on such perfection that I refuse to acknowledge anyone else as a Christian. If I did, there would be no one in the Church, because we all fall short of the ideal. There are many who have so far made only a little progress, but who shall not be rejected. So what am I saying? Surely that we must constantly run towards the goal, aiming for perfection. You cannot be half-hearted with God, obeying some of his Word and rejecting some at will. God always looks for integrity as the most important ingredient of worship; real singleness of mind, without show or sham – impossible with a divided heart. The spiritual start of a good life comes when our inner feelings are truly focused on God, as we cultivate holiness and justice. While we are imprisoned in a body not one of us has enough strength to go ahead with the eagerness we ought to show, and the majority are so held back by weakness that hesitating, faltering and even falling they make little progress. But we must all go as far as we possibly can, and complete the journey we have begun. No one can travel so badly that he does not make some progress each day. So let us never give up. Then we shall move forward daily in the Lord's way. And let us never despair because of our limited success. Even though it is so much less than we would like, our labour is not wasted when today is better than yesterday! We must keep the goal in sight with real singleness of mind. We must not flatter ourselves nor indulge our vices, but try to improve all the time until we attain true goodness. If we spend our whole lives seeking and following, we shall eventually reach this goal when, released from the weakness of the flesh, we are welcomed into full fellowship with God.

Chapter 7

The sum of the Christian life: self-denial.

1. ... The first thing we must do is to hand ourselves over to God, and devote the total energy of our minds to his service. By service, I do not mean simply verbal obedience, but the state of mind which, stripped of carnal desires, implicitly obeys the call of God's Spirit. This transformation, which Paul calls the renewing of the mind (Eph. 4:23), was unknown to the philosophers of old, although it is the only way to true life. They made reason the sole ruler of man and listened only to her, as the arbiter of conduct. But Christian philosophy makes her move aside and give complete submission to the Holy Spirit, so that the individual no longer lives, but Christ lives and reigns in him (Gal. 2:20).

2. So follows the second principle, that we must not follow our own way but the Lord's will, and aim always to promote his glory. We are really succeeding when, almost forgetting ourselves and putting aside our own way of thinking, we genuinely try to obey God and his commandments. When Scripture tells us to put aside selfish interests, it not only removes undue desire for wealth, power or popularity from our minds, but wipes out all ambition for worldly glory, and other more secret temptations. The Christian ought to be disciplined to think that throughout his life he is dealing with God. Then he will bring everything to God for his assessment and use, as he looks only to him. The one who has learned to look to God in everything he does is simultaneously distracted from all empty thoughts. This is the self-denial which Christ emphasised so clearly to his disciples from the outset (Matt. 16:24). As soon as it grips the mind, it leaves no place for pride and ostentation. No room either for greed, lust, self-indulgence, effeminacy or other vices brought about by love of self ...

[3–4]

5. It is incredibly difficult to carry out our duty to seek our neighbour's good. Unless we stop thinking about ourselves, and in a way stop being ourselves, we will never achieve it. How can we display the love which Paul describes, unless we renounce ourselves, and devote ourselves totally to others? He says that 'Love is patient, love is kind. It does not envy, it does not boast, it is not proud. It is not rude, it is not self-seeking, it is not easily angered' (1 Cor. 13:4–5). Even if 'not self-seeking' was the only thing required of us, by nature we would not have a hope of fulfilling it. By nature we are inclined to love only ourselves. Nature does not allow us blithely to overlook our own interests and look to those of others, still less spontaneously to relinquish our rights and pass them on to others. But Scripture, in guiding us to this position, reminds us that whatever we receive from the Lord is given on condition that we use it for the good of the whole Church. The right use of our gifts is warmly and generously to share them with others. The simple truth upon which we need to learn and act is that all the talents we possess are divine deposits, entrusted to us for the sole purpose of benefiting others. Scripture goes even further when it compares these gifts with different members of the body (1 Cor. 12:12). No member exists for its own benefit, but for fellow-members. Whatever the believer can do, he must do for his brethren, not looking to his own interests in any way, except to do his utmost for the building up of the whole Church. So let this be our way of showing goodwill and kindness, as we realise that in everything which God has given us we are his stewards and must give account of our stewardship. Further, the only right way is the way of love, as we put our neighbour's advantage above our own …

6. So that we shall not get tired of doing good (as would undoubtedly be the case otherwise) we must add the other

quality in Paul's list: 'Love is patient, love is kind … it is not easily angered' (1 Cor. 13:4–5). The Lord commands us to do good to everyone without exception, even though the majority don't deserve it. Scripture adds a splendid reason, when it tells us that we are not to think about what men deserve in themselves, but to look at the image of God which exists in everyone, and to which we all owe honour and love. The same rule should be even more carefully observed in those who are of the household of faith, since that image is renewed and restored in them by the Spirit of Christ. It doesn't matter who the person is needing your help: you have no excuse for refusing it. Say he is a stranger: the Lord, in renewing the image of God in him, has given him a mark which ought to be familiar to you, so he forbids you to despise your own flesh (Gal. 6:10). Say he is humble and little thought of: the Lord points to him as one in whom his own image shines (Isa. 58:8). Say you feel no ties of obligation towards him: the Lord puts him in his own place, so that you may realise the great obligation you are under to him. Say he is totally unworthy of any efforts you may make for him. The image of God, which commends him to you, is worthy of everything in you, and anything you can do. Even if he is totally undeserving, and has also angered you by hurt and wrong-doing, there is no valid reason why you should not enfold him in love and load good deeds upon him (Matt. 6:14; 18:35; Luke 17:3). He deserves something very different from me, you may well say. But what has the Lord deserved? As we think of him, we can achieve the difficult and unnatural: we can love those that hate us, give good for evil, and blessing for cursing (Matt. 5:44), remembering that we are not to dwell on the evil in men, but look to the image of God in them. This image covers and obliterates their faults, and by its beauty and dignity draws us to love and to embrace them.

7. So we shall succeed in denying ourselves if we fulfil these duties demanded by love. However, they are not fulfilled

simply by discharging them completely. They must be done from a motive of pure love. It is possible to carry out every sort of good deed, as far as the external act goes, but not to do it in the right way. Some people might be thought very generous, and yet give insult by superior looks or cruel words. It is sad that in these days most men dispense charity in a patronising way. Such behaviour is unworthy, even among unbelievers, but something much more is required of Christians. It is not even enough for them to have a cheerful manner or to carry out their duties with courteous speech. First, they must put themselves in the place of the one who needs assistance, and sympathise with his misfortune as though they felt and suffered it themselves. Only then will a feeling of pity and humanity move them to help him just as they would themselves. The person who has this attitude will assist his brethren without spoiling the act by arrogance and blame. Even more, he will not look down on the brother to whom he does a kindness, as one who needed his help, or put him under obligation. There is a parallel in the body, where all the members work together to compensate for a weak or diseased member. This is only natural. So, a person who has carried out one kind of duty will not think he can sign off. This often happens when a rich man, after giving away a certain sum, leaves the rest to others as though he had no further interest. Really everyone should think that he owes himself to his neighbours, and that the only limit to his generosity is the end of his resources.

Chapter 8

Bearing the cross: one part of self-denial.

1. The godly mind must climb higher still: to where Christ calls his disciples when he says that each one must take up his cross (Matt. 16:24). Those whom the Lord has chosen and honoured with his friendship must be prepared for a

hard, strenuous and testing life, full of many different troubles. It is the Father's will to exercise his followers in this way, putting them to the test. He put Christ his first-born through the course, and has continued it with all his children. Though his Son was precious to him above everyone else, and he was 'well pleased' in him (Matt. 3:17; 17:5), yet we know that, far from being treated gently and indulgently, his whole life was an unremitting cross. The apostle gives the reason: 'Although he was a son, he learned obedience from what he suffered' (Heb. 5:8). Why should we spare ourselves the state to which Christ our head saw fit to submit, especially since he did so on our behalf, so that he could display a perfect pattern of endurance? The apostle declares that all God's children are destined to be conformed to him (Rom. 8:29). All this is a great comfort in hard and difficult circumstances, which people consider trying and miserable, because we realise that we are sharing fellowship with Christ in his suffering. As he rose to the glory of heaven through a vale of tears, so we too are led there through various tribulations. Paul says 'We must go through many hardships to enter the kingdom of God' (Acts 14:22) and again, 'I want to know Christ and the power of his resurrection and the fellowship of sharing in his sufferings, becoming like him in his death' (Phil. 3:10). The bitterness of the cross for us is sweetened greatly when we think that the more we suffer hard experiences, the more sure we are made of our fellowship with Christ. By communion with him not only are our sufferings blessed to us, but they further our salvation in no small measure.

2. The only thing which made it necessary for our Lord to bear the cross, was to prove his obedience to the Father. But there are many reasons which make it necessary for us to live constantly under the cross. We are so feeble by nature and so quick to think we are perfect that we need visible demonstration of our weakness. Otherwise, we think we are much better than we are, and are sure that we can

triumph over all difficulties. So we indulge in stupid confidence in the flesh. This even makes us proud before the Lord, as if we could cope without his grace. He stamps on this arrogance when he proves to us by experience how great our weakness is. So he allows us to meet with disgrace, poverty, bereavement, disease or some other affliction. Then, feeling overwhelmed, we admit defeat and humbly call on him for strength, which alone enables us to cope. Even the holiest of men would feel too secure in their own strength, if they were not made to know themselves more thoroughly by the trial of the cross. David realised this when he said, 'When I felt secure, I said, "I shall never be shaken." O Lord, when you favoured me, you made my mountain stand firm; but when you hid your face, I was dismayed' (Ps. 30:6–7). He confesses that in prosperity his feelings were dulled, so that, neglecting God's grace, he looked to himself and claimed unending life. If this happened to such a great man, surely we should be doubly careful? When things go well, we flatter ourselves that we are very steady and patient, but when we are humbled by hardship, we realise that this is just not so. Only then will believers make progress in humility, abandon all confidence in the flesh, and throw themselves upon God's grace. When they have done this, they experience the reality of his power which is all sufficient.

3. Paul teaches that tribulation brings about patience, and patience character (Rom. 5:3–4). God has promised that he will be with believers in tribulation, and they feel the truth of his promise. Supported by his hand, they can endure with patience. This would be impossible in their own strength. Patience gives believers experimental proof that God really does provide the help which he has promised, whenever need arises. So their faith is strengthened, because it would be most ungrateful not to believe that God's truth, already experienced, will also be found firm and reliable in the future. Now we can see how many advantages

result from the cross. It overturns the high opinion we have of our own virtue and exposes the hypocrisy we so often indulge in. It removes our deadly confidence in the flesh, teaching us, when humbled, to rest in God alone, so that we are not discouraged or depressed. Then we learn that victory is followed by hope, because the Lord, fulfilling his promise, establishes his truth for the future. If for no other reasons, it is obvious that we must bear the cross. It is vital to get rid of self-love and be made aware of weakness. Then, convinced of our weakness, we distrust ourselves. This makes us switch our confidence to God, looking to him with such total confidence that we know we can rely on his help. Then by his grace we shall stand firm to the end, realising that he is true to his promises, and so sure of this that we can be strong in hope.

4. Another purpose the Lord has in afflicting his people is to try their patience and train them in obedience. Of course they can only be obedient to him as he enables them, but through it he draws out convincing proof of the graces he has conferred upon his saints. Otherwise they would remain hidden away and unused. So, as he brings into the open the strength and steady endurance with which he has provided his servants, he is said to be trying their patience! ...

5. We still do not see how essential obedience is until we realise how easily our fleshly nature shakes off God's yoke whenever we have had a time of ease and indulgence. It is the same with frisky horses, which become uncontrollable when they have been idle for a few days. They no longer recognise the rider whose command they had previously obeyed implicitly. So we invariably become like the people of Israel of whom God has to complain, 'Jeshurun [Israel] grew fat and kicked; filled with food, he became heavy and sleek. He abandoned the God who made him' (Deut. 32:15). God's kindness should attract us and make us aware of his goodness, but such is our sinful nature that we always

seem to deteriorate when indulged. Because of this, we need to be restrained by his discipline from behaving like spoilt children. By means of the cross, the Lord acts when necessary to prevent us from being arrogant in material prosperity, proud when we are honoured, or puffed up with any other advantages of body, mind or fortune. We could so easily become offhand and he has to curb the pride of life in us as he sees best. We don't all suffer from the same disease, so we don't all need the same cure. Therefore we are not all disciplined by the same kind of cross. The heavenly physician treats some gently and others with harsher remedies. His aim is to provide everyone with a cure, so no one is left out, because he knows that all of us, without a single exception, are diseased.

6. Our gracious Father wants not only to prevent weakness, but to correct past faults and so keep us in the way of obedience. So whenever we are afflicted, we ought to look back over our lives right away. Then we shall realise that the sins we have committed deserve such punishment. But the call to patience is not to be based mainly in the acknowledgment of sin. Scripture cites a far better reason when it says that when things go wrong 'we are being disciplined so that we will not be condemned with the world' (1 Cor. 11:32). So in the misery of testing times we ought to recognise God's kindness, because in it all he is furthering our salvation. He afflicts us not to ruin or destroy, but to deliver us from the condemnation of the world ...

Chapter 9

Meditation on the future life.

1. Whatever sort of tribulation we suffer, we should always remember that its purpose is to make us spurn the present and reach out to the future. God knows very well that we

are naturally drawn to love this world. So, to keep us from clinging to it too closely, he finds good reason to call us away and wake us up. You would think that heaven and immortality would be the height of our ambition through life. We should be ashamed to be no better than the animal world, since our hope of life beyond the grave is the only thing which makes their position lower than ours! But when we look at men's plans, desires and actions, there seem to be nothing but earthly values. How stupid we are! Our minds are so dazzled with the glare of wealth, power and honours, that we cannot see beyond them. The heart also, preoccupied with greed, ambition and lust, is in the grip of worldly attractions, and looks for happiness only here on earth. To combat this disease, the Lord makes his people aware of the futility of their present life by frequent proof of its misery. So that we don't have false hopes of deep and lasting peace, he often allows us to be disturbed by war, riots, burglary and a variety of other disasters. So that we don't get over-ambitious for wealth that doesn't last or rely on what we already have, he reduces us to poverty or, at least, a modest income. So that we don't become selfishly preoccupied with married life, he even allows us to be saddened by the foolish behaviour of our partners, the wickedness of our children or the trauma of bereavement. If we are spared this, he still has to keep us from pride and complacency. He shows us by illness or accident how all human advantages are flimsy and fleeting. We profit by the discipline of the cross when we realise that this life is, in itself, restless, troubled and unhappy. Even its so-called blessings are uncertain, passing, empty and tinged with evil. From all this, we have to conclude that the best we can hope for here is a struggle. When we think of the crown of life, we must look up to heaven. We must realise that our minds never genuinely long for future joy until they have learned to make little of this present life.

2. There are no half-measures in all this. Either we must have a very low opinion of this life or be trapped by an excessive love of it. If we have any thoughts about eternity, we must fight hard to throw off this bondage. Because this life has so many attractions and apparently much to enrich us, it is vital from time to time to be drawn away from its fascinations. If even the constant spur of affliction fails to make us aware of our wretched state, what on earth would happen if we had a life of uninterrupted success and joy? Awareness that this life is like smoke or a shadow is not confined to scholars. It is common knowledge among ordinary people. Even so, we are to think about it as little as possible and make plans as though life here was for ever. If we happen to see a funeral, or wander in a graveyard, we cannot help being aware of death and philosophising eloquently on the emptiness of this life. But this is very momentary and we forget it all immediately we move on. We not only forget death but also mortality itself, lying back in comfort as though we could expect life here to go on endlessly. If anyone reminds us that man is only here for a brief spell, we agree but pay little attention, inwardly convinced of our indestructibility! So we must all agree that it is vital to be made aware, by experience, of the misery of this earthly life. Otherwise we go on gazing at it with mindless admiration, as if it contained everything that is good. If God finds it necessary to discipline us in this way, surely we must listen when he calls and shakes us out of lethargy? Then we shall be quick to despise the world and aspire wholeheartedly to the future life.

3. The contempt which believers should train themselves to feel for this life, must not make them hate it or be ungrateful to God. This life is full of much unhappiness, but we must also recognise it as a blessing from God. If we do not recognise God's kindness to us, we are indeed ungrateful. Certainly for believers life is proof of divine benevolence, since its purpose is to secure their salvation. Before God

shows us openly our inheritance in glory, we are aware of him as Father by lesser proofs, that is, the blessings he showers on us each day. So since this life makes us acquainted with the goodness of God, we must not scorn it as though it contained nothing good. Even if there were no indications in Scripture (and there are many), nature itself spurs us on to thank God for bringing us to birth, allowing us to live and preserving us here on earth. An even stronger motive is to realise that we are prepared here for the glory of God's kingdom. The Lord has ordained that those who will one day be crowned in heaven must have fought the good fight here on earth. There can be no triumph until we have overcome in the struggle of this life and gained the victory. Another reason for gratitude is that we begin to experience, in various ways, a foretaste of divine blessing so that our appetites are whetted for the full experience. When we have discovered that our earthly life is a gift of God's mercy, which we need to remember with gratitude, we can then come down to assessing its wretchedness accurately. So we shall get away from the undue attachment to which we naturally incline.

Chapter 10

How to use the present life and its comforts.

1. Scripture gives us plenty of teaching about the proper use of earthly blessings and as we plan our lives, we must not ignore it. If we are to live at all, of course we need certain essential supports. But we should not exclude many things which seem to have more to do with pleasure than necessity. We must find a happy medium, so that we use everything in the right way, with a clear conscience. The Lord makes this clear in his Word, when he tells us, his people, that this life is a kind of pilgrimage through which we press on to the heavenly kingdom. If we are only passing through

we must, of course, use temporal blessings only as long as they assist our progress and do not hinder us. So Paul, with good reason, urges us to use this world without abusing it, and to buy possessions as if we were selling them (1 Cor. 7:30–31). This world is a slippery place and there is real danger of falling, so let us set our feet where we can stand securely. There have been some good and holy men who when they saw constant overindulgence wanted to curb and correct it, but thought that there was no other way than to allow men only the bare necessities. This is godly advice but unnecessarily severe, because it binds our consciences in closer fetters than they are bound by God's Word. Also necessity, according to them, meant abstinence from anything desirable, so that bread and water was the rule. Others were even more austere, like Cratetes the Theban, who threw his wealth into the sea, because he thought that it would destroy him. At the opposite extreme, many today look for an excuse for excessive self-indulgence in the use of material things. They take for granted that their liberty must not be restrained in any way, but that it should be left to every man's conscience to do whatever he thinks right. I agree that conscience should not be bound by rigid laws, but because Scripture has laid down general rules for the use of material possessions, we should keep within the limits laid down.

2. So our principle should be that we are not using God's gifts wrongly when we use them for the purpose for which they were intended, since he created them for our good and not our destruction. This will keep us on the right path. If we think out the reason for the creation of food, we will realise that it was not only for necessity, but for our enjoyment and delight. So with clothing, the purpose was not only necessity but beauty and honour. With herbs, fruits and trees, there are grace and perfume as well as usefulness. If this was not so, the Psalmist would not list among God's mercies, 'wine that gladdens the heart of man, oil to

make his face shine' (Ps. 104:15). The Scriptures would not
mention frequently, in reference to his kindness, that he
had given such things to us. The natural qualities in his creation often show how they can be rightly enjoyed. Has the
Lord given flowers great beauty and perfume, and then
made it wrong for us to enjoy it? Hasn't he given us colours
to enjoy and qualities in material things like gold and silver,
ivory and marble which make them precious? To sum up:
he gives many things a value apart from their usefulness.

3. So let's get rid of the inhuman philosophy which only allows necessities. Not only does it wrongly deprive us of
legitimate enjoyment of God's generosity, but it cannot be
effected without depriving man of all his senses, reducing
him to a block. On the other hand, we must guard carefully
against the lusts of the flesh, which if not restrained break
all bounds and are advocated by those who, in the guise of
liberty, allow themselves all kinds of licence. There is an
automatic check when we recognise that the aim of creation
is to teach us to know the Creator and feel gratitude for his
generosity. It is hardly gratitude if you gorge and stupefy
yourself with food and drink so that you are unfit to pray or
do your work. There can be no recognition of God if the
flesh, boiling with lust because of extreme indulgence, in-
fects the mind with impurity and makes it lose discernment
of what is upright and true. There is no thankfulness to God
for our clothes, if we have such splendid things that we ad-
mire ourselves and look down on others. Also the love of
show and luxury can pave the way for immodesty. We fail
to recognise God when all these things capture and dazzle
our minds. Many people are so set on indulging the senses
that their minds lie buried. Many are so obsessed with marble, gold and pictures that they become marble-hearted,
are changed into hard metal or become like painted figures.
The kitchen, with its savoury smells, occupies so much of
their time that they have no spiritual savour. And so we
could go on. So it is obvious that it is essential we should re-

strain licentious abuse and live to Paul's rule, ' ... Do not think about how to gratify the desires of the sinful nature' (Rom. 13:14). Where too much liberty is allowed, there is no limit or restraint.

4. The safest and quickest way of achieving such restraint is by despising the present life and aspiring to eternal life. Two rules then emerge. First, 'those who have wives should live as if they had none' and, 'those who use the things of the world, as if not engrossed in them' (1 Cor. 7:29, 31). Second, we have to learn to be just as calm and patient in enduring poverty as we are moderate in enjoying plenty. The person who makes it his aim to use the world as if it barely existed will cut out gluttony, effeminacy, ambition, pride and ostentation, but more than this he will cut out all the cares which would hinder him from gaining eternal life. Cato rightly said that 'luxury causes great care and produces great carelessness as to virtue'. There is an old proverb which says that 'those who are much occupied with the care of the body usually give little care to the soul'. So while the liberty of Christians must not be regulated by strict rules, it is always subject to the law that they must indulge as little as possible. It must be their constant aim to cut out all unnecessary luxury and extravagance and beware of letting a help become a hindrance.

5. Another rule is that those in restricted circumstances should learn to put up with their wants patiently. They should not long too much for material things, since moderation is a sign of significant progress in the school of Christ. The person who is resentful of poverty nearly always goes overboard in prosperity. Someone who is ashamed of a poor dress will usually be too proud of a splendid one. Someone who resents a simple meal will overindulge when he can afford it. A person who cannot accept a humble position, will be boastful of position should it arise. All who have a genuine longing for holiness must learn from the

apostle's example, 'whether well fed or hungry, whether living in plenty or in want' (Phil. 4:12). Scripture has a third rule for ensuring right use of earthly blessings. It makes clear that they have all been given by God's kindness and in trust, so that we will have to give account one day. So we must employ them as if we could hear 'Give an account of your stewardship' constantly ringing in our ears. At the same time, we should remember the one who will take account. It is the Lord who commends abstinence, sobriety, frugality and moderation and condemns luxury, pride, ostentation and vanity. He approves the way of life which displays true charity, and disapproves of all pleasures which deflect the heart from chastity and purity, or darken the intellect.

[6]

Part X

JUSTIFICATION BY FAITH

Chapter 11

Justification by faith defined.

1. I hope I have now shown clearly that man's only hope of escaping the curse of the Law and finding salvation lies in faith. I have also tried to show what the nature of faith is, the benefits it brings, and the results it produces. It can all be summed up like this: Christ is given to us by the goodness of God; we grasp and possess him by faith; then we obtain a twofold benefit. First, when we are reconciled by the righteousness of Christ, God becomes a gracious Father instead of a judge. Second, when we are sanctified by his Spirit, we reach after integrity and purity of life. This second benefit, i.e. new birth, has been fully discussed. The subject of justification was discussed more briefly, because it was important to explain first that the faith by which alone (through God's mercy) we obtain free justification, is not without good works. We also had to show the true nature of these good works. So now we must fully discuss the doctrine of justification, realising that it is the most important basis of true religion, and deserves close attention. Unless you understand first of all what your position is before God, and the judgment he has to pass on you, you have no foundation on which salvation can be built or on which true godliness can flourish. The need to understand the subject will become very clear as we proceed.

2. So that we don't get confused from the start, let me first explain the meaning of the expressions 'to be justified by faith, or, by works'. A person is said to be justified in the sight of God when in the judgment of God he is considered

righteous and is accepted because of that righteousness. Because sin is abhorrent to God, the sinner cannot find grace in his sight so long as he is regarded as a sinner. Wherever sin exists, there also is the wrath of God. Conversely the person who is justified is no longer regarded as a sinner, but as righteous, and so stands acquitted at the judgment seat of God, where all sinners are condemned. Just as a man, deemed innocent by an impartial judge, is said to be justified, so a sinner is said to be justified by God when he asserts his righteousness. In the same way a man can be said to be 'justified by works' if there is a purity and holiness in his life which deserves the affirmation of righteousness at the throne of God, or if by the perfection of his works he can satisfy the divine justice. On the other hand, a man will be 'justified by faith' when, quite apart from the righteousness of works, by faith he lays hold of the righteousness of Christ. Then he can appear in the sight of God not as a sinner, but as righteous. So we simply interpret justification as the acceptance with which God receives us into his favour as if we were righteous: this justification consists in the forgiveness of sins and the imputation of Christ's righteousness.
[3–6]

7. The apostle Paul maintains that the power of justifying exists in faith, not on its own account, but only because faith receives Christ. For if faith justified in itself, or by its own intrinsic virtue, because it is always weak and imperfect it could only be partly effective, and so our righteousness would be damaged and only allow us partial salvation. Obviously we don't hold this view, but know that God alone can justify. Christ was given to us for righteousness, but we cannot receive Christ unless we come empty and with a heart open to receive his grace. To say that faith is needed to receive Christ is not to deny that the power to justify us lies in Christ alone. There is no reason why faith, though in itself of no status or value, should not justify us by

giving Christ, just as a clay vessel filled with coins may give wealth. So I say that faith, which is only the instrument for receiving justification, must not be confused with Christ, who is the actual cause, as well as the Author and minister of this great blessing. This deals with the problem of how the term 'faith' must be understood when we consider justification.
[8–15]

16. When Scripture talks of justification by faith, it urges us to turn away from our own works and look only to the mercy of God and the perfection of Christ. The order of justification is set out like this: first, God in his freely given goodness is pleased to embrace the sinner in his wretchedness, because he sees him entirely devoid of good works. The cause of this kindness lies in God alone. Then God influences the sinner by an awareness of his goodness, making him distrust his own works and cast himself totally upon God's mercy for salvation. This is the nature of the faith by which the sinner obtains salvation and becomes aware that he has been reconciled by God. He knows that by Christ's intercession he has obtained pardon for sin and is justified. Finally he realises that, although he has been renewed by God's Spirit, he must not look to his own efforts but solely to the righteousness treasured up for him in Christ ...

17. Here we must remember the link we established before between faith and the Gospel: faith is said to justify because it receives and embraces the righteousness offered in the Gospel. The very fact that it is said to be offered by the Gospel means that works are excluded. Paul repeatedly declares this and demonstrates it clearly in two particular passages. In the epistle to the Romans, comparing the Law and the Gospel, he says, 'Moses describes in this way the righteousness that is by the law: "The man who does these things will live by them." But the righteousness that is by faith says ... if you confess with your mouth, "Jesus is Lord," and be-

lieve in your heart that God raised him from the dead, you will be saved' (Rom. 10:5–6, 9). The distinction between the Law and Gospel is obvious: the former gives justification to works whereas the latter bestows it freely without any help from works. This is a vital passage of Scripture, and it can free us from many difficulties once we realise that the justification given us by the Gospel is free from any terms of Law. Because of this, Paul more than once places the promise in stark opposition to the Law. 'For if the inheritance depends on the law, then it no longer depends on a promise' (Gal. 3:18). There are other similar expressions in the same chapter. Undoubtedly the Law also has its promises, so there must be a difference between the promise of the Gospel and the promise of the Law. It is this: the promises of the Gospel are entirely undeserved and based simply on God's mercy, whereas the promises of the Law depend on works ...

21. We must now see how justification by faith means reconciliation with God, and that this consists entirely in the remission of sins. We have to keep returning to the truth that the wrath of God is on everyone, as long as they remain sinners. Isaiah puts it so clearly. 'Surely the arm of the Lord is not too short to save, nor his ear too dull to hear. But your iniquities have separated you from your God; your sins have hidden his face from you, so that he will not hear' (Isa. 59:1–2). We are told here that sin separates God and man; that his face is turned away from the sinner and that this is inevitable since contact with sin is abhorrent to God's righteousness. In the same way Paul shows that man is at enmity with God until he is restored to favour by Christ (Rom. 5:8–10). So when the Lord admits someone to union with him, he is said to justify him because he cannot accept him or be united with him without changing his state from that of a sinner into that of a righteous man. This is done by remission of sins, because if those whom the Lord has reconciled to himself are judged by works, they will still prove to be

sinners. It is obvious that the only way in which those whom God calls are made righteous, is by having their corruption washed away by the remission of sins. This is what justification means.
[22]

23. There is no doubt that it is entirely by the intervention of Christ's righteousness that we obtain justification before God. This is equivalent to saying that man is not just in himself, but that the righteousness of Christ is communicated to him by imputation, when really he deserves punishment. So we can dismiss the absurd dogma that man is justified by faith because it brings him under the influence of God's Spirit, by whom the sinner is made righteous. This could never be reconciled to the doctrine mentioned first. The one who is taught to seek righteousness out of himself obviously cannot already possess it in himself. This is clearly expressed by Paul when he says that he who knew no sin was made an atoning sacrifice for sin, that we might be made the righteousness of God in him (2 Cor. 5:21). You can see that our righteousness is not in ourselves, but in Christ, and that the only way we can possess it is by being made partakers with Christ, since we possess all riches with him.

There is no conflict in this other reference: 'God ... sending his own Son in the likeness of sinful man to be a sin offering ... condemned sin in sinful man, in order that the righteous requirements of the law might be fully met in us' (Rom. 8:3–4). Here the only fulfilment to which he refers is what we acquire by imputation. Our Lord Jesus Christ communicates his righteousness to us, and in some wonderful way transfuses its power into us.

He makes this point again: 'For just as through the disobedience of the one man the many were made sinners so also through the obedience of the one man the many will be made righteous' (Rom. 5:19). To state that we are held to be righteous, solely because the obedience of Christ is imputed to us as if it were our own, is simply to place our righteousness in the obedience of Christ ...

Chapter 12

We must lift up our minds to God's judgment seat, in order to be persuaded of his free justification.

1. Although the truth of this doctrine is abundantly proved by Scripture, we cannot see clearly how essential it is until we establish the basis on which the discussion ought to rest. First, we must remember that the righteousness we are looking at is not of a human tribunal, but of a heavenly one. We must beware of using our own paltry standards to estimate the perfection needed to satisfy God's justice. It is amazing how rash and presumptuous we can be in defining it. The ones who are most sinful seem to be the ones who talk most glibly about the righteousness of works. They do this because they are not focusing on the righteousness of Christ. If they did they would never insult him so. His righteousness is so complete that it cannot accept anything less perfect and pure. Man never has reached and never will reach his standard. It is easy for scholars to talk of the sufficiency of works for justification, but when we come into God's presence all such talking ceases. The discussion is real and no longer a superficial dispute. We must really apply our minds if we are to find a satisfactory answer to this matter of true righteousness. The question must be, 'How shall we answer the heavenly Judge when he calls us to account?' We must meditate on him as he is portrayed in Scripture, not in our puny little minds. His is a brightness which hides the stars, a strength which melts the mountains, an anger which shakes the earth, a wisdom which outstrips all intellectuals, a purity which makes everything seem impure, a righteousness beyond the angels and a vengeance which reaches the deepest hell. If men's actions are to be judged, who could feel safe before God's throne? ...

The discussion of this subject will be completely useless, unless we come before the heavenly Judge longing for acquittal, and humble ourselves freely, admitting our worthlessness.

2. So we must look upwards and learn to tremble instead of to exult. When we compare ourselves with others, it is easy to pride ourselves on our virtue, but when we look to God, our confidence evaporates. The position of the soul in relation to God is very like that of the body to the universe. Our physical eyes are pleased with their vision when looking at things close to, but when they look directly at the sun they are dazzled and overwhelmed by the brilliant light. Then they realise just how weak they are. So we may think ourselves superior to, or equal with, other men, but this means nothing to God and it is his judgment alone which counts. We must not deceive ourselves with false confidence or he will have to say to us, as he did to the Pharisees, 'You are the ones who justify yourselves in the eyes of men, but God knows your hearts. What is highly valued among men is detestable in God's sight' (Luke 16:15). You can still boast, but God will turn away. The true servant of God, one truly taught by his Spirit, will say, 'Do not bring your servant into judgment, for no-one living is righteous before you' (Ps. 143:2); or perhaps, 'how can a mortal be righteous before God? Though one wished to dispute with him, he could not answer him one time out of a thousand' (Job 9:2). Here we are clearly told what the righteousness of God is. It is a righteousness which no human efforts can satisfy, which makes us guilty of a thousand sins, and excuses none. Paul had the right idea when he said: 'My conscience is clear, but that does not make me innocent. It is the Lord who judges me' (1 Cor. 4:4).
[3–4]

8. In conclusion, if we want to respond to the call of Christ, we must get rid of all arrogance and self-confidence. The

first springs from an illusion of self-righteousness, when a man thinks that there is something in himself which deserves God's commendation. The latter may exist even without a dependence on good works. Many sinners, enjoying the pleasures of life to the full, never think of God's judgment. They are overcome by lethargy and can't be bothered to think about God's mercy. It is vital to get rid of such apathy if we are to turn to Christ. Then, realising our own emptiness, we can be filled with his blessings. We shall never have sufficient confidence in him, unless we distrust ourselves totally. We shall never take courage from him until we despair of ourselves. We shall never find comfort in him until we stop looking for it in ourselves. When we have got rid of all self-confidence and trust only in the certainty of his goodness, we are ready to grasp and lay hold of the grace of God ...

Chapter 13

Two things to be observed in free justification.

[1–2]

3. If we try to find out how the conscience can be squared before God, we shall find that the only way is by having his righteousness freely given to us. It is good to remember Solomon's words, 'Who can say, "I have kept my heart pure; I am clean and without sin"?' (Prov. 20:9). There isn't a single person who is not full of vice of one sort or another. If the most perfect man looks into his conscience, will he feel calm and satisfied that everything is well between him and God? Will he not rather be attacked by tormenting thoughts, as he sees the grounds for condemnation in himself? When it looks at God, conscience must either be completely at peace or full of the terror of hell. There is no point in talking about righteousness, unless it is secure enough to

support us before the throne of God. When the soul can come boldly into his presence and hear his judgment without fear, then we shall know we have at last found true righteousness. Paul has good reason to stress this: 'For if those who live by law are heirs, faith has no value and the promise is worthless' (Rom. 4:14). First he states that faith is empty if the promise of righteousness has anything to do with our works, or depends on obeying the Law. No one could rest safely in that, because we could never be sure that we had satisfied the Law; certainly good works aren't enough. We have only to look at our own lives. Hypocrisy can plunge the mind of a man into a dark abyss, when he believes his own self-flattery instead of God's verdict. It is as if he wants to relieve God of his office as judge. A very different state of mind fills the believer who sincerely examines himself. We would all falter and despair if we had to weigh up for ourselves how far we had progressed. Faith would be wiped out, because true faith means we do not vacillate and vary. It should mean that we have total security of mind, and somewhere utterly safe to stand. [4–5]

Chapter 14

How justification begins and progresses.

1. Now we must see what kind of lifelong righteousness it is possible for man to have ... In the first place, when men are judged by natural gifts, not an atom of good will be found anywhere unless Scripture is to be judged false. It describes all the sons of Adam by such terms as these: 'The heart is deceitful above all things and beyond cure' (Jer. 17:9). ' ... every inclination of his [man's] heart is evil from childhood' (Gen. 8:21). 'The Lord knows the thoughts of man; he knows that they are futile' (Ps. 94:11). 'All have turned aside, they have together become corrupt; there is no-one

who does good, not even one' (Ps. 14:3). Briefly they are termed 'flesh'. This name includes everything listed by Paul: adultery, fornication, uncleanness, lasciviousness, idolatry, witchcraft, hatred, disputes, wrath, strife, seditions, heresies, envyings, murders, drunkenness, revellings and every sort of filth and abomination it is possible to imagine (Gal. 5:19–21). This then is the worth of which we can boast! Even if there is someone who seems full of integrity and virtue, because God does not look at the outward, we must go to the heart of things if we are to assess how far works can secure righteousness.

2. I am not denying that the excellent traits we see in unbelievers are divine gifts. And I am not so stupid as to maintain that the justice and uprightness of Titus and Trajan were no better than the rage and cruelty of Caligula, Nero and Domitian. The controlled behaviour of Vespasian was much to be preferred to the obscene lusts of Tiberius. The observance of law and justice must be better than flouting them. There would be chaos in this world if justice and injustice were to be confused. God rewards those who live good lives with many material blessings. It isn't that the outward appearance of virtue merits his favour, but he wants to show how much he rejoices in true righteousness. So he rewards even the outward show of righteousness. It is obvious that all virtues are gifts of God, since everything praiseworthy comes from him.

3. Augustine's comment is true, that all who are strangers to the true God, however excellent they may be, deserve punishment if only because they contaminate the pure gifts of God. Though they are God's instruments to preserve human society by justice, control, friendship, moderation, courage and wisdom, they carry out these good works of God in the worst possible way. They are kept from wrong, not by a sincere love of goodness, but merely by ambition

and self-love, or some other wrong motive. So because these actions are polluted at the very source by impurity of heart, they cannot be called virtues simply because they resemble them. We must remember that the object of righteousness is the service of God: nothing else will do. The ungodly may perform acts which seem good, but their motives are evil because they are not seeking to serve God. So their deeds are sinful …
[4–8]

9. When God reconciles us to himself by the righteousness of Christ, he grants us the free pardon of sin and regards us as righteous. His goodness is linked with mercy, so that he lives in us by means of the Holy Spirit, by whose influence the lusts of our flesh are daily put to death and we are sanctified. Our lives are consecrated to the Lord, and we aim at purity of life as our hearts are disciplined to obey the Law. Our greatest desire becomes to obey his will, and in everything to see his glory promoted. But even when we walk in the ways of the Lord, under the guidance of the Holy Spirit, we are still aware of enough failure to keep us humble. ' … There is no-one who does not sin' (1 Kgs 8:46). What righteousness can be gained by works? The best we can manage is spoilt by sin. If a saint of God tried to choose the action which he thought finest in his whole life, he would still find something rotten in it. The smallest blemish is an offence to God, so even the saints cannot do a single thing which, if judged on its own merits, does not deserve condemnation.

10. Even if it was possible to behave perfectly, one sin is enough to wipe out all previous righteousness (Ezek. 18:24). James agrees with this: 'For whoever keeps the whole law and yet stumbles at just one point is guilty of breaking all of it' (Jas. 2:10). Since this mortal life is never completely free of sin, whatever righteousness we managed to gain would eventually be destroyed by subsequent sin. It

could not stand God's scrutiny, and so be imputed to us for righteousness. Whenever we assess the righteousness of works, we must look to the commandment and not just isolated works. When righteousness is claimed by the Law, it is useless to produce one or two single deeds. We must show non-stop obedience. God does not grant us forgiveness of our past lives, so that we may then seek righteousness in the Law. This would only mock us with false hopes. Since perfection is altogether unattainable as long as we are in the flesh, and the Law pronounces death and judgment on all who have not attained perfect righteousness, there will always be good reason to accuse and convict us unless God intervenes in his mercy. Only he can absolve us by the constant remission of sins. So our earlier statement stands: if we are judged by our own worthiness, in everything that we think or plan with all our efforts, we deserve death and destruction.

11. We must emphasise two things. No believer ever performed a single deed which, if tested by God's strict justice, could escape condemnation. Second, even if he could, because the deed is tainted by his sins it is stripped of all merit ...
[12–17]

18. When in Scripture believers constantly comfort themselves with reminders of their own purity and goodness, and even talk about it, it is done in two ways. Either they feel triumphant by comparing themselves with the ungodly who will, of course, be condemned, or a clear conscience gives some comfort and security even before God. We shall look at the first category again later, but now as we look at the second, let it remind us that we can have no confidence in works at the bar of God, and we cannot glory in any opinion of their worth. Believers must turn their eyes to the goodness of God alone. It is not only an initial turning, but an abiding rest. When true conscience is established, of

course good works follow, because they are proof of God living in us. But confidence in works has no place unless you have first put your whole confidence in God's mercy. The Christian must not turn back to the merit of works as a prop to salvation, but must depend entirely on God's free promise of justification. But of course every believer is strengthened in his faith by signs of God's favour towards him. When we remember the gifts which God has bestowed on us, they are like rays from the divine countenance, by which we are enabled to see the bright light of his goodness. So it is with the gift of good works, which shows that we have received the spirit of adoption.

19. When believers feel their faith strengthened by an awareness of integrity, and experience feelings of great joy, it is because the fruits of Christian living convince them that the Lord has admitted them to his family ... But even fear of God does not bring total security and the saints are always aware that integrity is tainted. But as evidence of the new birth gives proof of the Holy Spirit within, and because they have experienced God as Father in this, they are encouraged enormously to look for his help in everything. They would not be able to do this if they had not already realised that God's goodness is ensured by his promise alone. If they try to measure it by their good works, they will wallow in uncertainty. These works in themselves provoke divine displeasure by their imperfection as well as his favour for their burgeoning purity ...

20. So it is right that believers have no confidence in works. We must not claim any merit, because the works are God's gift to us, evidences of his goodness to us. We must not detract from the free righteousness of Christ, since this is the sole ground of our confidence ...
[21]
[Chapter 15]

Chapter 16

Objections in this doctrine refuted.

1. There are some irreverent theologians who accuse us of destroying good works when we say that men are not justified by them. They say also that we make the means of justification too easy when we say that it consists in the free remission of sins. Their allegation is that justification by faith destroys good works. But an examination of their lives shows no great zeal for good works save that when faith is so highly extolled, works are deprived of their proper position. We would say that, on the contrary, they are given greater prominence. We do not promote a faith devoid of good works, nor a justification which can exist without them. The difference is that while we acknowledge that faith and works cannot be separated, we know that justification is based on faith, not works.

This becomes clear when we turn to Christ alone and direct our faith to him, deriving his power in return. Why are we justified by faith? Because by faith we grasp the righteousness of Christ which alone can reconcile us to God. But you cannot have faith without holiness because 'It is because of him that you are in Christ Jesus, who has become for us wisdom from God – that is, our righteousness, holiness and redemption' (1 Cor. 1:30). Christ does not justify anyone without also making him holy. It is an inseparable bond. Those whom he enlightens, he redeems; those whom he redeems, he justifies; those whom he justifies, he sanctifies. Justification and sanctification are inseparably bound up in Christ. Do you want justification in Christ? You must first possess Christ. But you cannot possess him without sharing in his sanctification. Christ cannot be divided. Because the enjoyment of these blessings comes through him, he gives both at once and you cannot have one without the other. So we see how true it is that we are justified not without, and yet not by, works. It is by sharing in Christ, that we are justified, and this sharing includes sanctification no less than justification.

Chapter 17

The harmony of promises of the Law and the Gospel.

[1–7]

8. ... Because Paul knew that justification by faith was the refuge of those who lacked their own righteousness, he emphasised that all who are justified by faith are excluded from the righteousness of works. But because it is obvious that this justification is common to all believers, he also emphasises that no one can be justified by works. Indeed, justification is entirely without the assistance of works. However, it is one thing to assess the power inherent in works and quite another to decide their place after justification by faith has come about. If we evaluate works according to their inherent value, we must realise they are unfit to stand in God's presence. Man has no works to make him boast before God, and he must be justified by faith alone. We define justification like this: when the sinner is admitted into communion with Christ, he is reconciled to God for his sake; when purged by his blood he obtains the remission of sins, and then clothed with his righteousness he stands secure before the judgment seat of heaven. Because forgiveness of sins has already been granted, the good works which follow have a different value, because all their imperfections are covered by Christ's perfection. All taint is wiped out by his purity, and there will be no divine condemnation. So the good works done by believers are considered righteous, that is, they are imputed for righteousness.
[9]

10. By this reasoning we can agree with our opponents that there is partial righteousness in works. Even more, we can say they are approved by God as if they were absolutely perfect. If we remember the foundation on which this all rests, every problem is solved. A work only becomes acceptable when it is received with pardon. This can only be when God looks on us, and all that belongs to us, as in Christ. Just as we appear righteous before God when we are grafted into Christ, because our sins are covered with his innocence, so do our works. God reckons them as righteous works. He does not hold against them all their impurities, because these are buried by Christ's purity. Not only we but also our works are justified by faith alone. If righteousness of works depends on faith and free justification and is produced by it, it is all included in the package of the doctrine of justification ...
[11–15]
[Chapter 18]

Chapter 19

Christian freedom.

[1]

2. Christian freedom seems to consist of three parts. First, the consciences of believers, while seeking the assurance of justification before God, must rise above the Law, and no longer attempt to obtain justification by it. For while the Law leaves no one righteous, we must either be cut off from all hope of justification, or be free from the Law in such a way that no account at all is taken of works. Anyone who imagines that he can obtain justification by works in any way has an endless task, because he is debtor to the whole Law. We must rest in the mercy of God alone, turning from

ourselves and looking only to Christ. The question is not, 'How may we be righteous?' but, unworthy as we are, 'How may we be *regarded* as righteous?' If our consciences are to be reassured, they must give no place to the Law. This does not mean that believers do not need the Law. It teaches and encourages them to do good, although they do not make reference to it before the judgment seat of God. Our Christian lives should always be aiming at holiness because we are called to this (Eph. 1:4; 1 Thess. 4:3). The function of the Law is to motivate us to purity and remind us of our duty. But when the conscience feels anxious about God's approval, it is not the requirements of the Law which are relevant, but Christ who surpasses all the perfection of the Law. He alone is our righteousness.
[3]

4. The second part of Christian freedom is this. Consciences obey the Law not just because they have to; when they are free from the yoke of the Law, they obey the will of God voluntarily. When they are in terror of the Law, they do not obey God so swiftly. Let me explain. The commandment says, 'Love the Lord your God with all your heart and with all your soul and with all your strength' (Deut. 6:5). To do this, the soul must be free of every other thought or feeling and the heart cleansed from all selfish desires. There must be concentration on the one goal. Even those who seem to have made a lot of progress in the Christian way still fall far short. Although they love God in their mind and with a sincere heart, the lust of the flesh holds them back, despite all their efforts. If they look to the Law, they can see that everything they attempt is doomed. No one can deceive himself by saying that his actions are not all bad and the good will be accepted by God. The Law demanding perfect love condemns all imperfection. Our 'partly good' works break God's Law by virtue of being imperfect.
[5–6]

7. The third part of our Christian freedom is to realise that we are not bound to observe outward regulations concerning unimportant matters. We are free to observe them or not. Without this freedom our consciences will never be able to rest. There must be free choice over what we eat, what we wear and which days we observe as holy. This is a more important issue than one might think. If conscience gets wrongly entangled there is an endless maze from which it is hard to escape ... The most trivial things can become matters of debate and make us frightened to move. All that matters is that God approves, and we must avoid the opposite dangers of despairing of or despising his favour.

8. Paul says, 'I am fully convinced that no food is unclean in itself. But if anyone regards something as unclean, then for him it is unclean' (Rom. 14:14). So he agrees that we are free before God to choose in non-essential matters. Superstitious scruples contaminate things which God meant for our good. So the apostle adds, 'Blessed is the man who does not condemn himself by what he approves. But the man who has doubts is condemned if he eats, because his eating is not from faith; and everything that does not come from faith is sin' (Rom. 14:22–3). Fear can prevent us from receiving God's gifts with thanksgiving and so they remain unsanctified (1 Tim. 4:5). Thanksgiving proceeds from a mind which recognises the kindness and goodness of God. We must use his gifts without unnecessary scruples of conscience, so that we may be at peace with him and recognise his generosity. The same applies to all optional religious ceremonies. They are all right if they build us up in our faith, but not if we feel under a moral obligation to observe them.

9. However, we must remember that Christian freedom is a spiritual matter. Its whole purpose is to give peace to trembling consciences, whether they are anxious about forgiveness of sins, imperfect actions or the exercise of choice.

It is quite wrong to interpret it as an excuse for lust, so that God's gifts are abused, or to use it in such a way that it stumbles weaker brethren. The materialism of the present age is an obvious example. Those whose means allow it live in luxury, enjoying food, clothes and housing which must keep up with the Joneses! A man glories in those things and defends them under the pretext of Christian freedom. He calls them non-essentials – and so they are, as long as he does not consider them essential. But when they are lusted for, boasted about and indulged in excess, things which in themselves are lawful become defiled. Paul makes the distinction well: 'To the pure, all things are pure, but to those who are corrupted and do not believe, nothing is pure. In fact, both their minds and consciences are corrupted' (Titus 1:15). Why does Jesus pronounce a woe on the rich who have already received their consolation (Luke 6:24)? Why do Amos and Isaiah pronounce judgment on the rich who bask in luxury (Amos 6:1, 4; Isa. 5:8, 12)? Of course ivory, gold and wealth are God's good gifts, permitted, indeed designed by his Providence for man's use. Laughter, good food and drink, possessions and music have never been forbidden. But wrong use can be made of them all if we wallow in luxury and constantly seek new pleasures. God's gifts must be used in moderation, without pride or arrogance. Moderation allows legitimate use: without it even ordinary pleasures can become excessive. A proud mind can live in modest clothes, and true humility be cloaked with fine linen. So everyone must remember that God's gifts are for life, not luxury. We must all learn with Paul the law of Christian freedom, to be content with our lot. He 'learned to be content whatever the circumstances' (Phil. 4:11).
[10–16]

Part XI

PRAYER

Chapter 20

Prayer. The chief exercise of faith, by which we daily receive God's benefits.

1. We have already seen how man is completely devoid of good in himself, and without any means of gaining his own salvation. If he wants help in that situation, he has to go outside himself and find it elsewhere. We have explained how the Lord lovingly and spontaneously manifests himself in Christ, and in him offers us happiness for misery and plenty for need. He opens up the treasures of heaven to us, so that we can turn in joyful faith to his beloved Son, depend on him, rest in him and cling to him in full assurance. This is a hidden philosophy which cannot be discovered by logical argument and can be understood only by those whose eyes God has opened to see light in his light. We learn by faith that God supplies whatever we need in Christ Jesus and that we may draw from him as from an inexhaustible fountain. Then we proceed to pray for what we have learned to be available in him. If we know God as the sovereign giver of all good, who invites us to pass on our requests, and yet we don't bother to come to him, it won't help us one bit. It is as if we had been told about some buried treasure but allowed it to stay in the ground. So the apostle, to show that faith unaccompanied by prayer cannot be genuine, puts things in this order: as faith springs from the Gospel, so by faith our hearts are influenced to call upon the name of God (Rom. 10:14). Paul speaks, too, of the Spirit of adoption, which seals the testimony of the Gospel on our hearts, gives us courage to make our requests known to God, causes groanings which cannot be uttered,

and enables us to cry '*Abba*, Father' (Rom. 8:15, 26). We have only touched on this last point briefly, so now we must look in more detail.

2. Prayer enables us to explore the riches which are treasured up for us with our heavenly Father. There is real contact between God and men when they enter the upper sanctuary, appear before him and claim his promises. We learn by experience that what we believed merely on the authority of his Word is true. There is nothing that we can expect from the Lord, for which we are not also told to pray. Prayer digs up the treasures which the Gospel reveals to the eye of faith. The need for prayer, and its usefulness, cannot be emphasised too much. The Father declares rightly that our only security lies in calling on his name, because by doing this we are asking him, by his Providence, to look after us. His power will strengthen us in our weakness, his goodness will keep us in his favour, sinful as we are, and we can ask him to reveal himself to us in all his perfection. So deep peace and tranquillity are given to our consciences. When we lay our burdens before the Lord, we can rest in complete assurance that none of our problems is unknown to him, and he is able and willing to provide for us in the best way.

3. You may well ask why, if God already knows our difficulties and what is best for us, we need to plead with him in prayer. It is as if he were asleep and had to be woken up by the sound of our voices! This argument ignores the reason the Lord has taught us to pray. It is not for his sake, but ours. He wants us, rightly, to give due honour to his name by acknowledging that everything comes from him. But even in this, the benefit is ours. The saints of old found that the more confidently they proclaimed the mercies of God to themselves and others, the stronger was the urge to pray. Elijah is a good example: when he was sure of God's plan, he had good reason to assure Ahab of the promise of rain,

and yet he prayed earnestly and sent his servant to check seven times (1 Kgs 18:42–3)! He didn't doubt the promise, but knew it was his duty to tell God of his longings, in case his faith became sluggish. It is true that when we are quite oblivious to our need, God still protects us and helps unasked. But it is very much in our interests to be constantly in prayer. This ensures that our hearts are always eager to love and serve him, every time we turn to him as our anchor in need. Second, it ensures that we need never be ashamed of the desires and longings which come into our minds as we expose them before him and pour out our hearts to him. Finally, we learn to receive all his blessings with true gratitude as we remember in prayer that everything comes from him. When we receive what we asked for and know that he has answered our prayers, we long for his favour even more, and have even greater joy in enjoying the blessings we receive. Experience confirms the assurance of his Providence; we realise that his promises will never fail us and he freely allows us access in every time of need. We know that his hand is always stretched out to help his people in practical ways. Although our heavenly Father never slumbers nor sleeps, he often seems to do so, in order to train us in prayer. Instead of being idle and indifferent, we have to pray earnestly to our lasting good …

4. The first rule of true prayer is to have heart and mind in the right mood for talking with God. We shall achieve this if we put aside all carnal thoughts and worries which would distract us from direct and pure contemplation of God. Our minds must be wholly concentrated on prayer and raised above themselves. This does not mean we shall have no anxious thoughts; indeed, it is often these that make our prayer fervent. So we see that holy men of God often display great anguish when their cries reach the Lord from a deep abyss. I am trying to say that all irrelevant worries, which distract the mind, must be driven out. Otherwise our thoughts are drawn away from heaven to grovel on earth.

We must not bring into God's presence anything which our blind and stupid reason works out, nor must our minds be kept within the bounds of our own petty vanity, but rise to a level of purity worthy of God.

5. Everyone who professes to pray must concentrate all his thoughts and feelings and not be distracted by random ideas. Nothing prevents the reverence due to God more than frivolity which betrays a mind prone to license and without fear. We have to work very hard at a difficult task. No one is able to concentrate on prayer so hard that distracting thoughts do not break in, either breaking the train of thought or hindering the prayer by a digression. Surely we realise how wrong it is, when God allows us to talk freely with him, to abuse the privilege by mixing sacred and secular things because reverence for him is not sufficient to control our minds? We treat prayer like conversation with an earthly friend, allowing our thoughts to roam all over the place. We must understand that the only ones who prepare themselves for prayer adequately are those who are so impressed with God's majesty that they can be free from all earthly worries and affections. The habit of lifting up our hands in prayer is designed to remind us that we are far away from God, unless our thoughts rise to heaven. 'To you, O Lord, I lift up my soul' (Ps. 25:1) reminds us of this, and Scripture frequently uses the expression 'to raise our prayer', meaning that those who want to be heard by God must not grovel in the mire. The more generously God deals with us, inviting us to unload our burdens on to him, the less excuses we have for ignoring such an incomparable blessing. Prayer must outweigh everything else and make us appreciate it so much that it occupies all our thoughts. This can only happen when we let our minds rise upwards, fighting every obstacle.

The second guideline must be that we should only ask what God allows. Although he tells us to pour out our hearts (Ps. 62:8), he does not include giving way to stupid and depraved desires. When he promises to grant believers their requests, he does not intend to indulge our slightest whim.

People fail constantly in this. Not only do many (without any modesty or reverence) pray about superficial things, but they arrogantly bring their selfish dreams before the throne of God. Some are so silly that they pester God with desires which are so vile they would hesitate to mention them to their friends.

... Because it is hard to reach the high standard God requires, we need help. As the eye of our mind should be fixed on God, so our heart's affection should follow. But both fail in this and go in the wrong direction. To help us in our weakness, God gives us the guidance of his Spirit in our prayers, to show us what is right and control our desires, because 'the Spirit himself intercedes for us with groans that words cannot express' (Rom. 8:26). Not that he actually prays or groans, but he arouses in us sighs and longings and assurance which our natural powers could never bring about. Paul has good reason to use the phrase 'with groans that words cannot express' for prayers made under the guidance of the Spirit. Those who are really wrestling in prayer are aware that anxiety can hold them back and confuse them, so that they hardly know what to say. To pray aright is a special gift.

This is not to encourage laziness or carelessness by leaving everything to the Holy Spirit. Some people wrongly say that we must wait until he takes over our minds; we are merely trying to say that, despairing of our own lack of enthusiasm, we should long for the Spirit's help. When Paul urges us to pray in the Spirit (1 Cor. 14:15), he is still telling us to be active ourselves. He implies that while the inspiration of the Spirit is necessary for effective prayer, it doesn't stand in the way of our own efforts. Indeed God is concerned to see how much faith influences our hearts.

6. Another condition of prayer is that, in asking, we must

be sincerely aware of our needs. Many people repeat prayers in a half-hearted way and following a set form, as if they were carrying out some task for God. Even though they see prayer as a necessary remedy, it still seems as though they pray out of a sense of duty, with cold hearts and not much thought. Some vague feeling of need makes them pray, but does not seem to have any connection with specific needs. Worst of all, could there be a greater insult to God than the force of asking forgiveness of sins when there is no sense of sin? Mankind is full of depravity and much is taken for granted without reference to God's magnanimity. There is another sin which is almost as bad: that is when people mutter prayers unthinkingly, with some vague idea that God is pleased with prayer. Believers should be specially careful not to come into God's presence without serious intention. Even in things we ask for the glory of God and not our own satisfaction, we must have really earnest longing. So when we pray that God's name should be hallowed, we must really hunger and thirst for the answer.
[7]

8. The third rule of prayer is that the one who comes into God's presence to pray must get rid of all boasting and self-opinionated ideas. Self-confidence must be thrown aside and God be given all the glory. Pride always means turning away from God. The holier the servant of God, the lower he will bow down in the presence of the Lord. So Daniel, who was highly commended by the Lord, says, 'We do not make requests of you because we are righteous, but because of your great mercy. O Lord, listen! O Lord, forgive! O Lord, hear and act! For your sake, O my God, do not delay, because your city and your people bear your Name' (Dan. 9:18–19). He is not speaking in a general sense but makes it quite clear it is a confession of personal sin as well as the sin of his people Israel ...

9. A plea for forgiveness, with humble and sincere confession of guilt, must be the prelude to all true prayer. The holiest of men cannot hope to get anything from God until he has been freely reconciled. God cannot look favourably on anyone who has not been pardoned ... Although the saints of old do not always seem to ask forgiveness in specific terms, if we study their prayers as given in Scripture, we shall see that their boldness in prayer was derived solely from God's mercy. They always started by begging his pardon. If a man looks to his conscience, far from putting all his troubles before God unthinkingly, he would be afraid to approach at all, if it were not for God's mercy and forgiveness ...
[10]

11. The fourth rule of prayer is that, despite the necessary humbling, we should be spurred on to pray with real confidence of success. The two things are perfectly consistent, if we are aware that it is only the goodness of God which lifts the contrite sinner. As we have seen before, repentance and faith go hand in hand, indissolubly linked, the one causing fear and the other joy. Both are present in true prayer ... The confidence I refer to does not free the mind from all anxiety nor calm it with a lovely sense of rest. This is the privilege of those who are not worried by care, tortured with regret or alarmed by fear. But the best stimulus the saints have to prayer is when driven by necessity and anxiety, in despair their faith comes to their aid just at the right time. In their distress, God's goodness shines on them in such a way that, while they are weighed down by their troubles and haunted by fear of the future, they can still trust him. This makes the present bearable and hope of deliverance one day assured. It is essential for both elements to be present in the believer: there must be awareness of need and trust in God. God must be grieved when we ask without expecting any reply. Prayer is not a casual matter; we have to show the faith Christ commands when he says,

'Therefore I tell you, whatever you ask for in prayer, believe that you have received it, and it will be yours' (Mark 11:24) and again 'If you believe, you will receive whatever you ask for in prayer' (Matt. 21:22) ... It is faith that obtains answers to prayer. This is what Paul conveys in that well-known passage, 'How, then, can they call on the one they have not believed in? And how can they believe in the one of whom they have not heard? ... Consequently, faith comes from hearing the message, and the message is heard through the word of Christ' (Rom. 10:14, 17). He gradually argues the origin of prayer from faith, clearly stating that God cannot be truly called upon except by those who, by the preaching of the Gospel, have experienced his mercy and love.

[12–52]

Part XII

GOD'S ELECTION AND MAN'S DESTINY

Chapter 21

Eternal election. By which God has predestined some to salvation and others to destruction.

1. The Gospel is not preached to everyone, and among those to whom it is preached does not always meet with the same response. This difference demonstrates the unsearchable depths of divine judgment, and is subordinate to God's purpose of eternal election. If we suggest that salvation is offered to some and not others simply to suit God's pleasure, enormous question marks arise. These questions are unanswerable unless we hold correct views on election and predestination. This is a puzzling subject to many, because it is hard to square the thought of some men being predestined to salvation and others to destruction. I hope to show that they are needlessly confused. In the very complexity of the matter, we can discern the outworking of the doctrine and its happy outcome. We will never be convinced as we ought, that our salvation flows from God's free mercy, until we understand eternal election. God's grace is illustrated by the fact that he does not give away salvation indiscriminately, but gives to some what he denies to others. Ignorance of this great truth detracts from God's glory and prevents true humility. Paul maintains that the principle can be understood only if works are set on one side and God is seen to elect those whom he has predestined. His exact words are, 'So too, at the present time there is a remnant chosen by grace. And if by grace, then it is no longer by works; if it were, grace would no longer be grace' (Rom. 11:5–6). If we have to go back to the origin of election to make it obvious that salvation springs from God's mercy

alone, those who try to banish the doctrine are wrongly obscuring what they ought to emphasise, and eradicating true humility. Paul clearly states that it is only when salvation is attributed to undeserved election that we can know God saves whom he wills of his own good pleasure. He is under obligation to no one. There who try to keep people from the doctrine are unfair to God and man alike, because there is no other way to humble us or to make us realise what we owe him. There is no other sure ground for confidence. We say this on Christ's authority. To deliver us from fear and make us invincible in the dangers and battles of this life, he promises safety to all whom the Father has taken into his keeping (John 10:28–9). All who do not know they are God's special people must be miserable and in constant fear. So those who ignore the advantages of which we have spoken destroy the basis of salvation and do everyone a disservice. Surely this is how the Church is made known to us. Since, as Bernard rightly teaches, it cannot be found in the created world, because it lies hidden in the sacred lap of predestination.

Now I want to talk to two different groups of people. The subject of predestination, which is difficult enough already, is made even more puzzling and dangerous by human curiosity. This cannot be held back from forbidden areas, even floating up to the clouds in a determination to discover all the secret things of God. When we see decent men rushing into such presumption, we must point out how wrong it is. First, when they delve into the question of predestination, they must remember that they are probing the depths of divine wisdom, and if they dash ahead too boldly, then instead of satisfying their curiosity they will enter a maze with no exit! It is not right that men should pry into things which the Lord has chosen to conceal in himself, or gaze at the glorious eternal wisdom which he wants us to worship, not understand. In this way his perfection will be more clearly seen. The secrets of his will which he sees fit to make plain, are revealed in his Word: everything necessary for our well-being is there.

2. We have come into the way of faith [says Augustine], so let us keep to it. It leads to the King's rooms, where all the treasures of wisdom and knowledge are hidden. For our Lord Jesus Christ said, even to his closest disciples, great and most select disciples, 'I have much more to say to you, more than you can now bear' [John 16:12]. We must go on, advancing and growing, so that we may understand the things we cannot yet understand. But if we are still journeying when the last day comes, we shall learn then what we could not understand here on earth.

If we seriously consider that the Word of the Lord is the only guide to our understanding of him, it will prevent all presumption. We shall realise that the moment we go beyond the limits of Scripture, we shall be off course, in the dark and stumbling. Our first aim must be to know only the doctrine of predestination as set out in God's Word. Otherwise we delude ourselves. We need not be ashamed to be ignorant in an area where to realise our ignorance is to be learned. But we must steer clear of any search after knowledge which it would be stupid and dangerous to follow. If a fertile imagination urges us on, we must counter it with the words, 'It is not good to eat too much honey, nor is it honourable to seek one's own honour' (Prov. 25:27). We should rightly be alarmed about presumption which could plunge us into ruin.

3. Some people urge that the subject of predestination should rarely, if ever, be mentioned and tell us to avoid any discussion of it like the plague. Although they are right in saying that such deep things should be treated with moderation, the natural mind is going to raise questions. To hold a balanced view we must turn to God's Word, where we shall find true understanding. Scripture is the Holy Spirit's school where everything we need to know is taught and

where nothing is taught that is unnecessary. It would be quite wrong to keep believers from the scriptural doctrine of predestination. We would deprive them of God's blessing and scorn his Spirit. The Christian should be open to everything that God has spoken and equally desist from questioning things he does not choose to reveal. As Solomon says, 'It is the glory of God to conceal a matter' (Prov. 25:2). This does not mean we should remain ignorant of important things. Moses states the distinction clearly: 'The secret things belong to the Lord our God, but the things revealed belong to us and to our children for ever' (Deut. 29:29). He urges the people to study the doctrine of the Law as God commands, but not to pry into secret things.

[4–6]

7. ... Scripture clearly proves that God, by his eternal and unchanging will, determined once and for all those whom he would one day admit to salvation and those whom he would consign to destruction. His decision about the elect is based on his free mercy with no reference to human deserving. Equally, those whom he dooms to destruction are shut off from eternal life by his perfect, but incomprehensible, judgment. With reference to the elect, God's call and justification are proof of election which will be completed in glory. The unbelievers are cut off from the knowledge of his name and the sanctification of his Spirit, a preview of their coming judgment. I shall not bother to refute some of the stupid ideas men have raised to overthrow predestination, but deal only with genuine queries.

Chapter 22

Scriptural proof of this doctrine.

1. Many people would deny all the points I have made, especially the free and undeserved election of believers, but it is irrefutable. They imagine that God makes distinction according to merit: from foreknowledge he gives the adoption of sons to the worthy and condemns those who are bent on evil. This view obscures the doctrine of election and gives it a different origin. It has had a lot of support in every generation. But the truth of God is too sure and clear to be shaken by citing human authorities. Some people, ignorant of Scripture, attack sound doctrine with intolerable anger and falsehoods. Because God chooses some and rejects others, they argue with him. But if the facts are true, what is the point of quarrelling with God? Experience proves my teaching to be true: that God has always been free to shower his grace on whoever he wants to. Men might just as well question why they are superior to ox and ass. Only God knows the reason. He could have made them dogs when he formed them in his own image. Do they expect the lower animals to protest to God about the injustice of inferiority? Just as men enjoy privilege acquired without merit, so God also distributes favours according to his wishes ... When Paul states that we were chosen in Christ before the foundation of the world (Eph. 1:4), he makes it clear that there is no regard for our own worth. We were adopted into our heavenly inheritance in Christ because in ourselves we were incapable of such attainment. Elsewhere he exhorts the Colossians to give thanks that they had been made fit to share in the inheritance of the saints (Col. 1:12). If election precedes the divine grace which makes us fit for immortal life, what does God see in us to persuade him to elect us? Another passage makes this even clearer. God 'chose us in him before the creation of the world to be holy and blameless in his sight. In love he predestined us to be

adopted as his sons through Jesus Christ, in accordance with his pleasure and will' (Eph. 1:4–5). Here God's good pleasure is put in contrast to any possible worth in us. [2]

3. As surely as God's will prevails, good works are never taken into account. Paul makes this clear: God 'has saved us and called us to a holy life – not because of anything we have done but because of his own purpose and grace. This grace was given us in Christ Jesus before the beginning of time' (2 Tim. 1:9). The additional words 'called us to be holy', remove any doubt. If you say that God could foresee who would be holy and therefore elected them, you invert Paul's order. So we may safely infer that if he elected us to make us holy, he did not elect us because he saw that we *would* be holy. The two things are obviously contradictory, i.e. that the saints owe their holiness to election, but can attain election by means of works. There is no force in the objection that some people raise, that the Lord bestows election taking into account future, not present, merit. When we say that believers are elected so that they might be holy, the clear implication is that such holiness has its origin in election. How can it be held that things derived from election are the cause of election? The apostle confirms this when he adds, 'according with his pleasure and will which he has purposed in himself' (Eph. 1:9). The expression God 'himself', is equivalent to saying that his decree was formed without any reference outside himself. So Paul adds that the sole object of our election is that 'we should be to the praise of his glory'. We would not give all the praise for our election to God, if it were not free and undeserved. It could not be so if God based it on the future good works of any individual. What Christ said to his disciples applies to all believers: 'You did not choose me, but I chose you' (John 15:16). He not only excludes past merits, but maintains that they had nothing in themselves for which they could be chosen except what he knew he was to do in mercy. How are we

to understand Paul's words, 'Who has ever given to God, that God should repay him?' (Rom. 11:35). He obviously means that men are totally indebted to God's goodness going before, since there is nothing in anyone, past or future, to gain his favour.

[4–11]
[Chapter 23]

Chapter 24

Election is confirmed by God's calling. The reprobate bring upon themselves the righteous destruction to which they are destined.

[1–3]

4. When we look for assurance about our election, we should cling to those signs which are clear evidence of it. One of Satan's deadly weapons is to attack believers with doubts about whether they are among the elect, and then incite them to look for answers in the wrong way. In the wrong way means puny man trying to infiltrate the hidden depths of divine wisdom, going back to remotest eternity to discover what God has destined for him. So he falls into a huge abyss, gets entangled in endless snares and buries himself in thick darkness. The stupidity of the human mind has to be punished with destruction whenever it tries to aspire to divine wisdom in its own strength. It is a deadly temptation to which we are all prone. There is hardly anyone who does not think sometimes 'If my salvation comes only from God's election, what proof have I of that election?' When this thought dominates an individual, he will be permanently miserable, in terrible torment or mental confusion. The fact that these thoughts deprive a man of peace and rest in God is proof of their error. We must avoid them like the plague! Many regard the discussion of predestination as a dangerous

sea, but we can have a safe and tranquil journey if we do not rashly court danger. It is fatal to pry into God's eternal purposes, apart from his Word. But if we keep to the account of predestination in God's Word, then we shall find deep comfort. Our inquiry must begin and end with God's calling. Believers need to realise that daily blessings from God's hand have their origin in secret adoption. Isaiah writes, 'you have done marvellous things, things planned long ago' (Isa. 25:1). So we can be sure that God will impart as much of his wisdom as we need to know ...

5. If we are searching for God's fatherly love and grace, we must look to Christ, in whom alone the Father is well pleased (Matt. 3:17). If we are searching for salvation, life and immortality, we must turn to him again, since he alone is the fountain of life, the anchor of salvation and the heir of the kingdom. The purpose of election is no more than that, when we are adopted as sons by the heavenly Father, we will inherit salvation and eternal life through his favour. However much discussion goes on, this is the heart of the matter. Those whom God has adopted as sons, he is said to have elected not for themselves but in Christ Jesus (Eph. 1:4). He can love us only in Christ, and only, as partakers with him, honour us with the inheritance of his kingdom. If we are elected in him, we cannot find assurance of election in ourselves – indeed, not even in God the Father as seen apart from the Son. Christ is the mirror in which we can clearly observe our election. Since the Father has planned to graft into Christ's body all whom he wished to be his, and regards them as his sons, if we are in communion with Christ, we have proof clear and strong enough to show that our names are written in the Book of Life. He drew us into real communion with himself when by the preaching of the Gospel, he declared that he was given to us by the Father to be ours along with every blessing (Rom. 8:32). We are said to be clothed with him, to be one with him, so that we may live because he lives. The teaching is clear: 'For God so

loved the world that he gave his one and only Son, that whoever believes in him shall not perish but have eternal life' (John 3:16). He who believes in him is said to have passed from death to life (John 5:24). He calls himself the bread of life: if a man eats of it, he will never die (John 6:35). He is our witness that all who receive him by faith, will be regarded as sons by our heavenly Father. If we want more than that, we will have to go beyond Christ. But if that is our final goal, how futile it is to look elsewhere for what we have already found in him, and can only find in him. Anyway, as he is eternal wisdom, unchanging truth and has the mind of the Father, we need not fear that anything he tells us will differ from the Father's will, which we are trying to discover. He unfolds it truthfully to us, as it has been from the beginning and always will be. The effect of this doctrine ought to be seen practically in our prayers. Although assurance of election spurs us on to pray, it would be ridiculous to frame our prayer in words such as 'Oh Lord, if I am elected, please hear me!' He wants us to be at peace, satisfied with his promises and not to look elsewhere for our assurance. We shall be spared many a trap if we know how to use the written Word properly.

6. Something else to give us assurance is that our election is linked with our calling. Those to whom Christ reveals himself and welcomes into the heart of his Church, he takes into his care and protection. They are entrusted to him by the Father, to be kept to life eternal. Christ himself underlines this (John 6:37–9; 17:6, 12). If we want to know whether God cares about our salvation, we merely ask whether he has committed us to Christ, whom he has appointed to be the only Saviour. If we doubt whether we are accepted into Christ's protection, he deals with the doubt when he offers himself as our Shepherd, and states that we are among his sheep if we hear his voice (John 10:3, 16). So let us lay hold of Christ, who is lovingly offered to us, and comes out to meet us: he will number us among his flock

and keep us in his fold.

Then anxiety may arise as to our future status. As Paul teaches, those called were previously elected, so our Saviour says that many are called but few chosen (Matt. 22:14). Paul indeed warns against false confidence when he says, 'So, if you think you are standing firm, be careful that you don't fall!' (1 Cor. 10:12) and again 'But they were broken off because of unbelief, and you stand by faith. Do not be arrogant, but be afraid. For if God did not spare the natural branches, he will not spare you either' (Rom. 11:20–1). To sum up, we learn through experience that calling and faith are not much use without perseverance. But Christ has freed us from anxiety in this matter. The following promises obviously apply to the future: 'All that the Father gives me will come to me, and whoever comes to me I will never drive away', and 'this is the will of him who sent me, that I shall lose none of all that he has given me, but raise them up at the last day' (John 6:37, 39). Again, 'My sheep listen to my voice; I know them, and they follow me. I give them eternal life, and they shall never perish; no one can snatch them out of my hand. My Father, who has given them to me, is greater than all; no one can snatch them out of my Father's hand' (John 10:27–9), and 'Every plant that my heavenly Father has not planted will be pulled up by the roots' (Matt. 15:13). He makes it clear that those who are rooted in God can never lose their salvation. John's words confirm this: 'For if they had belonged to us, they would have remained with us' (1 John 2:19). Paul speaks of the tremendous triumph over life and death, things present and things to come (Rom. 8:38). This is all based on the gift of perseverance, and applies to all the elect. He says elsewhere, 'being confident of this, that he who began a good work in you will carry it on to completion until the day of Christ Jesus' (Phil. 1:6). When David's faith was in danger of failing, he prayed 'do not abandon the works of your hands' (Ps. 138:8). As Christ undoubtedly prays for all the elect, he asks for them what he asked for Peter, i.e. that their faith fail not (Luke 22:32). So we can infer that there is no danger of falling away, since the Son of God is never refused a request. When we are his, we are saved for ever.

7. Yet every day, those we thought belonged to Christ turn away from him. In the same passage that he declares that none of those whom the Father has given to him has perished, he makes the son of perdition an exception. This applies also to those who never followed Christ with the wholehearted confidence by which the certainty of election is established. John says, 'They went out from us, but they did not really belong to us. For if they had belonged to us, they would have remained with us' (1 John 2:19). I agree that there are certain characteristics similar to those of the elect, but they do not have the assurance of election which true believers find in the Gospel. So we mustn't let examples like this move us from quiet confidence in the Lord's promises, when he declares that all who receive him with real faith have been given him by the Father, and that none of them will perish (John 3:16; 6:39). Paul is not trying to keep Christians from assurance itself, but from flippant, worldly confidence which contains pride, arrogance and contempt of others. It prevents humility and reverence for God making a man forgetful of the grace he has received (Rom. 11:20). He is speaking to the Gentiles, showing them that they ought not to exult with pride and cruelty over the Jews whose place they take. He urges them to fear, but not to waver in alarm. They are to receive the grace of God humbly, but with full confidence in it ...
[8–17]

Chapter 25

The final resurrection.

1. Christ, the sun of righteousness, shines on us through the Gospel. After he had conquered death, he gave us the light of life (2 Tim. 1:10); so on believing, we are said to have passed from death to life (John 5:24), being no longer strangers and pilgrims, but fellow-citizens with the saints and of the household of God. He has made us sit with his only begotten Son in heavenly places (Eph. 2:6), so that we may be completely happy. But so that we do not resent the discipline of battle, we must look now at other teaching on the nature of hope. As we hope for what we cannot see (Rom. 8:25) and faith is the evidence of things not seen (Heb. 11:1), we are absent from the Lord as long as we are imprisoned in the body (2 Cor. 5:6). So Paul says, 'For you died, and your life is now hidden with Christ in God. When Christ, who is your life, appears, then you also will appear with him in glory' (Col. 3:3–4). But on earth we must 'live self-controlled, upright and godly lives ... while we wait for the blessed hope – the glorious appearing of our great God and Saviour, Jesus Christ' (Titus 2:12–13). We will need extraordinary patience if we are not to turn back, exhausted. All that we have said about salvation makes us raise our hearts to heaven so that, as Peter urges, though we do not see Christ now, yet believing we are 'filled with an inexpressible and glorious joy' (1 Pet. 1:8). Then we shall receive salvation, the fulfilment of faith. Paul says that the faith and love of believers are linked with the faith and hope reserved in heaven (Col. 1:5). When we keep our eyes fixed on Christ in heaven, and do not let anything on earth distract us, the promise 'where your treasure is, there your heart will be also' (Matt. 6:21), will be fulfilled. Now we can see why true faith is so rare: our lethargy makes it very difficult for us to overcome countless hurdles as we strive toward the prize of our high calling. A huge load of unhappiness al-

most overwhelms us and the scorn of unbelievers upsets us. We gladly give up the attractions of this life, but then seem to be chasing our elusive shadow as we seek for hidden happiness. Briefly, we feel under attack above and below, back and front, from fierce temptation. Our minds would be powerless to resist, unless they had been freed from earthly attachments and given to heavenly. We can only make real progress in the Gospel when we have acquired the habit of meditating all the time on the hope of resurrection.

2. Long ago, philosophers debated with each other as to what constituted ultimate good. Plato was the only one to acknowledge that it consisted in union with God, but even he could not form any idea of its true nature. This is understandable, since he knew nothing of the sacred bond of such union. We, even in our earthly pilgrimage, know what perfect happiness consists of. We long for it all the time, and it spurs us on until we attain it completely. As I said, no one can share in the benefits of Christ except those who lift their minds to the resurrection. This is the goal which Paul sets before all believers and at which they are to aim, forgetting everything until they reach it (Phil. 3:8). We must strive towards it, because if we are engrossed with the world, we shall suffer for our lethargy. Paul distinguishes true believers by this sign, that their conversation is in heaven, from whence they look for the Saviour (Phil. 3:20) ...

3. The importance of this matter ought to increase our enthusiasm. Paul rightly maintains that if Christ did not rise, the entire Gospel is fraudulent and useless (1 Cor. 15:13–17). Our state would be worse than other men's, because we are open to hatred and insult, incurring constant risks. We are like sheep destined for slaughter. So the power of the Gospel would be totally lost: there would be no adoption and no final salvation. When we have received Christ, the Author of perfect salvation, we must rise higher and realise that he is clothed in heavenly immortality and glory,

so that the whole body may be made conformable to the head. The Holy Spirit is always putting before us, in Christ, an example of the resurrection. It is hard to believe that after our bodies have disintegrated, they will rise again at the appointed time. Because of this, many philosophers agree that the soul is immortal, but few accept the resurrection of the body. We do not excuse this, but it reminds us that the matter is too hard for human understanding. To enable faith to overcome the difficulty, Scripture gives us two secondary proofs; one is the example of Christ's resurrection and the other the omnipotence of God. Now whenever the subject of the resurrection is under discussion, we can remember the Saviour, who, having completed his human life, gained immortality and is now the pledge of our future resurrection. In the troubles which beset us: 'We always carry around in our body the death of Jesus, so that the life of Jesus may also be revealed in our body' (2 Cor. 4:10). It is not right, or indeed possible, to separate him from us, without dividing him. Hence Paul's argument: 'If there is no resurrection of the dead, then not even Christ has been raised' (1 Cor. 15:13). He assumes it as an agreed fact, that when Christ was subjected to death, and in rising gained the victory over death, it was not on his own account only, but he had begun as the head what must surely be completed in all the members. Of course it would not be right to be made equal to him in every way. We read in Psalm 16:10, 'nor will you let your Holy One see decay.' The full effects of resurrection occurred only in Christ. Free from all corruption, he resumed a perfect form. So there can be no doubt about our sharing with Christ in a glorious resurrection. So that we may be happy with his promise, Paul clearly states that Christ sits in the heavens, and will come as Judge on the last day for the express purpose of changing our vile bodies, 'so that they will be like his glorious body' (Phil. 3:20–21). He also says that God did not raise Jesus from the dead as a single example of his great power, but that the Spirit has just the same effect on all believers. So the Spirit within

means life, because his purpose is to give life to our mortal bodies. These subjects deserve deeper study, but I hope my readers will find enough material to strengthen their faith. Christ rose again so that we might share with him in eternal life. He was raised up by the Father as Head of the Church, from which he cannot be separated. He was raised by the power of the Spirit, who does the same work of quickening in us. To sum it all up, he was raised up to be the resurrection and the life. As we have said, we can see a living image of our resurrection in this mirror. It gives certain proof to encourage our minds, so long as we don't give up. We must not get tired of waiting, because it is not our job to sort out God's timing. We rest patiently in him, until he brings in his kingdom in his own time. Paul refers to this when he comments, 'But each in his own turn: Christ, the firstfruits; then, when he comes, those who belong to him' (1 Cor. 15:23) ...
[4–12]

Part XIII

THE CHURCH

BOOK FOUR

OUTWARD MEANS BY WHICH GOD HELPS US. [HOW GOD INVITES US INTO COMMUNION WITH CHRIST AND KEEPS US THERE.]

Chapter 1

The true Church. (We should maintain unity with her, as the mother of all the godly.)

1. We have shown that Christ becomes ours through faith in his Gospel, so that we share in the salvation and eternal joy secured by him. Our ignorance, laziness and vanity are such that we need a great deal of help to bring us to living faith. We also need to grow in that faith. So God has made sure we have enough encouragement by entrusting his Gospel to the Church. He has appointed pastors and teachers to build up his people (Eph. 4:11) and has given them authority. He has not left out anything necessary to agreement in belief and to the right arranging of his Church. For instance, he has instituted sacraments which we know from experience are invaluable in strengthening our faith. Because we are confined in a body and have not yet reached angelic status, God has kindly made a way for us, who are so far removed from him, to draw near to him.

I will begin with the Church, the gathering of God's children, where they can be helped and fed like babies and

then, guided by her motherly care, grow up to manhood in maturity of faith. 'Therefore what God has joined together, let man not separate' (Mark 10:9). For those to whom God is a Father, the Church must also be a mother. This was true under the Law, and is true even after Christ's coming, since Paul stresses that we are the children of the new heavenly Jerusalem (Gal. 4:26).
[2–3]

4. The title, Mother, underlines how essential it is to know about the visible Church. There is no other way of entering into life unless we are conceived in her womb, brought to birth and then given her milk. We have to remain under her control until, at death, we become like the angels (Matt. 22:30). Our frailty ensures that we do not leave this school until we have spent our whole lives as pupils. Beyond the limits of the Church we can hope for no forgiveness of sins and no salvation. Isaiah and Joel make this clear (Isa. 37:32; Joel 2:32) and Ezekiel agrees when he declares, 'They will not belong to the council of my people or be listed in the records of the house of Israel' (Ezek. 13:9). Those who follow the way of true holiness are said to have their names written among the citizens of Jerusalem. So it is said in the Psalm,

> Remember me, O Lord, when you ... come to my aid when you save them, that I may enjoy the prosperity of your chosen ones, that I may share in the joy of your nation and join your inheritance in giving praise (Ps. 106:4–5).

In these words we see how God's fatherly love and the evidence of spiritual life are restricted to his own people. So abandoning the Church is always fatal.
[5–6]

7. I think our view of the visible Church has been made

sufficiently clear. Scripture speaks of the Church in two ways. Sometimes the reference is to the Church as it really is before God – the Church into which no one is allowed except those who have been adopted as sons of God and made true members of Christ by the sanctification of the Spirit. This includes the saints on earth and all the elect who have existed from the foundation of the world. Often the word Church refers to all those throughout the world who profess to worship one God and Christ, who have been baptised into the faith and who share in the Lord's Supper, professing unity in doctrine and love. They agree over belief in God's Word and observe the ministry appointed for preaching it. In this Church there is a large number of hypocrites who possess nothing of Christ except his name. Outwardly they seem all right, but they are ambitious, grasping, envious, evil-speaking men. Some lead even worse lives, but all are tolerated for a while, either because it is difficult to produce evidence of guilt or because there is weak discipline.

Of course we believe in the invisible Church, evident to God's eye alone, but we are also told to accept the visible Church and remain in communion with it.

8. Because it is important to recognise this Church, the Lord has distinguished it by specific marks or symbols. It is God's special prerogative to know those who are his, as Paul states (2 Tim. 2:19). This certainly acts as a brake on overconfidence, as we realise how far his judgments outstrip our understanding. Even those people who seem most wicked and beyond hope can be called back to life by his goodness, and seemingly stable characters can fall away. As Augustine says, 'In regard to the secret predestination of God, there are very many sheep outside, and very many wolves inside.' God knows, and has his seal on those who know neither themselves nor him. Of those who wear his badge, his eyes alone can see the truly holy ones, those who will persevere to the end, without which salvation is not

completed. However, he understands that to some extent we need to know the ones he regards as sons, and has acted accordingly. As absolute certainty is not essential, he has put loving assessment in its place. By this we acknowledge everyone as members of the Church who by confession of faith, consistency of behaviour and sharing in the sacraments, unite with us in acknowledging the same God and Christ. Because the knowledge of his body the Church is more necessary to our salvation, he has made it obvious by more definite signs.

9. So the visible Church is there for all to see. Wherever the Word of God is sincerely preached and listened to and wherever the sacraments are administered according to Christ's institution, we can be sure the Church of God exists because of his promise that 'where two or three come together in my name, there am I with them' (Matt. 18:20). Now to summarise this whole subject clearly. The Church universal is made up of the multitudes from every nation, who agree in the truth of divine doctrine and are united in a common faith. It includes single churches and single individuals as well as the general body, so long as the ministry of Word and sacrament are received ...

10. The preaching of the Word and the observance of the sacraments cannot happen anywhere without producing fruit and prospering because of God's blessing. I am not saying that wherever the Word is preached, there are immediate results, but that everywhere it is received and accepted there is always blessing. When the preaching of the Gospel is listened to reverently and the sacraments are observed, the Church is seen in truth and clarity; no one can with impunity reject her authority, ignore her rebuke, go against her advice or ridicule her judgment – far less revolt openly and destroy her unity.

The Lord sets such value on the fellowship of his Church that all those who deliberately cut themselves off from any

Christian group in which the ministry of Word and sacrament is faithfully upheld, are looked on by him as deserters. He commends her authority so highly that when it is flouted, he considers his own authority to be affected. The phrases used of the Church by Paul in 1 Timothy 3:15 have real meaning: 'God's household' and 'the pillar and foundation of the truth'. In these words Paul shows how the Church is the guardian of the truth, so that the world does not extinguish it. God has chosen to use her to preach his Word in all its purity and so he reveals himself to us as a parent, feeding us with spiritual nourishment and whatever we need for salvation. It is a tremendous privilege for the Church to have been chosen and set apart by Christ as his bride, 'without stain or wrinkle or any other blemish' (Eph. 5:27), and 'his body, the fulness of him who fills everything in every way' (Eph. 1:23). It follows then, that revolt from the Church is a denial of God and Christ. So it is all the more vital to beware of such a disastrous rebellion: it is tantamount to trying to destroy God's truth, for which we deserve to feel the full force of his anger. There could be no worse crime than blasphemously and shamefully breaking the sacred marriage bond, which the only begotten Son of God has condescended to make with us.

11. We must recognise the marks of God's Church, and see them through his eyes. Satan would love nothing better than to get rid of these characteristics, bring them into contempt and urge us into open revolt against the Church. His wiles ensured that for centuries the preaching of the Word disappeared, and now, with the same evil purpose, he is working to overthrow the ministry. Christ has so structured his Church, that if this is removed, the whole building will collapse. Now perhaps we can see how dangerous, even fatal, is the temptation to separate ourselves from the fellowship which shows the signs the Lord has chosen to characterise his Church. We need real discernment here. We must not be misled by the name 'Church': every group

which claims the name must be put to the test. If it maintains the practice instituted by the Lord in Word and sacraments, there will be no deception and we may safely respect it. If, on the other hand, there is no sign of these two marks, we must avoid such a sham.

12. When we say that the pure ministry of the Word and pure celebration of the sacraments are sufficient signs by which to recognise a Church, we mean that we should not write it off as long as these exist, even though it may be riddled with other faults. There may even be shortcomings in the administration of the Word and sacraments, but this should not cut us off from fellowship.

Doctrinal matters are not all of equal importance. Some are essential to true faith: for instance, that God is one, that Christ is God and the Son of God, that our salvation depends on God's mercy, and so on. There are other matters, which can be controversial, but do not destroy the unity of the faith. For instance, does it really matter whether one person believes that the soul flies to heaven when it leaves the body, and another maintains that all we can know for certain is that it is with the Lord?

The words of the apostle are, 'All of us who are mature should take such a view of things. And if on some point you think differently, that too God will make clear to you' (Phil. 3:15). The implication is that matters non-essential should not be the basis of argument among Christians. Of course it is good to have complete agreement, but as no one has perfect knowledge, we must either have no Church at all or forgive error in things which do not destroy the basis of salvation.

I am not condoning error, however trivial, nor trying to encourage it. I am trying to say that we should not leave a Church because of some minor fault, provided it maintains sound doctrine over essentials and practises the sacraments instituted by the Lord. Then we must try to change what is wrong.

Paul speaks of this in 1 Corinthians 14:30: 'And if a revelation comes to someone who is sitting down, the first speaker should stop.' Each Church member must do what is best for the majority, neither leaving the Church nor staying in it only to disturb its peace.

13. We ought to be much more tolerant about faulty behaviour. We can all fall into one of Satan's traps here: it is so easy to give a false impression of super holiness, as if we were already angels, and ignore the company of all who seem human in their shortcomings!

Others can sin more from thoughtless zeal than pride. When they see that, after people have heard the Gospel, their lives do not match up to their beliefs, they conclude that no Church exists at all.

Of course, we do not excuse shallow Christian living: it is far too common and the Lord has to correct it, especially if weaker consciences are offended. But it is also a sin to be unloving and unnecessarily severe. Such people imagine there is no Church unless there is complete purity and integrity of behaviour. Hating evil, they withdraw from a genuine Church, imagining that they are avoiding the company of the ungodly. They maintain that the Church of God must be holy, but they need to understand that it contains a mixture of good and bad. They should listen to the Saviour's parable in which he compares the Church with a net in which all kinds of fish are caught, but not sorted out until they are brought to land (Matt. 13:47–50). It is also compared with a field planted with good seed, in which an enemy scatters weeds; these are not separated until the harvest (Matt. 13:24–30). Finally, let those people look at the Church as a threshing ground where the wheat lies hidden under the chaff until, sorted by the fans and sieves, it is eventually stored in the granary (Matt. 3:12). If the Lord himself teaches that the Church will struggle with the burden of countless sinners until the day of judgment, it is obviously futile to look for a Church totally free from faults. [14–15]

16. Even genuinely good people are sometimes affected by this undue zeal for righteousness, though it is more usually the result of pride and a mistaken idea of holiness. Those in the forefront of inciting defection from the Church only want to demonstrate their own superiority by despising others. So Augustine wisely comments,

> Seeing that godly reason and the mode of church discipline ought specially to regard the unity of the Spirit in the bond of peace, which the apostle enjoins us to keep, by bearing with one another (for if we keep it not, the application of medicine is not only superfluous, but pernicious, and therefore proves to be no medicine); those bad sons who, not from hatred of other men's iniquities, but zeal for their own contentions, attempt altogether to draw away, or at least to divide, weak brethren ensnared by the glare of their name, while swollen with pride, stuffed with petulance, insidiously calumnious, and turbulently seditious, use the cloak of a rigorous severity, that they may not seem devoid of the light of truth, and pervert to sacrilegious schism, and purposes of excision, those things which are enjoined in the Holy Scriptures (due regard being had to sincere love, and the unity of peace), to correct a brother's faults by the appliance of a moderate cure.

His advice to the truly good person is lovingly to correct what he can, and put up patiently with what cannot be changed. This will cause distress, but God can transform the situation in this life, or at the final harvest root up the tares and scatter the chaff. It is possible to consider oneself an ardent champion of righteousness and yet rebel against the kingdom of heaven, which is the only kingdom of righteousness. God has chosen that the fellowship of his Church should be maintained in human society, and anyone who breaks its bonds, through hatred of the ungodly, embarks on a slippery slope, where there is great danger of cutting oneself off from the communion of saints. We must all realise that in a large company there may be several we have not been aware of, who are truly righteous and forgiven in the eyes of the Lord. Even of those who seem far from pure, there may be many who really are dissatisfied with themselves, and who sooner or later may be challenged by the Lord to greater integrity. We must remember that we have no right to pass judgment on a man for a single action, since the holiest person sometimes falls the worst. Let us also reflect that in the ministry of the Word and sharing of the sacraments, the power to gather the Church is too great to be negated by the faults of a few ungodly men. Finally, we know that, in judging the Church, God's opinion is far more important than man's.

17. Since the Church is rightly called holy, it is necessary to analyse such holiness. Otherwise, if we refuse to acknowledge any Church that is not absolutely perfect, we will have no Church at all! It is true, as Paul says, that Christ 'loved the church and gave himself up for her to make her holy, cleansing her by the washing with water through the word, and to present her to himself as a radiant church, without stain or wrinkle or any other blemish, but holy and blameless' (Eph. 5:25–27). But it is also true that the Lord is daily smoothing out the wrinkles and wiping away the spots. So it follows that the Church's holiness is not yet perfect. It makes steady progress, but is still imperfect. It advances constantly, but has not yet reached the goal. So when the prophets look ahead and say, 'Jerusalem will be holy; never again will foreigners invade her' (Joel 3:17) and 'it will be called the Way of Holiness. The unclean will not journey on it' (Isa. 35:8), they do not mean that no faults will be found in Church members, only that they will aim wholeheartedly for holiness and perfect purity. What they have not yet attained is, in God's goodness, attributed to them.

True holiness is all too rare, but we have to realise that the Lord has never been without his Church, and never will be until the end of time. Although the whole human race was corrupted by Adam's sin, God has always sanctified some to honour, so that no generation is without experience of his mercy. He has made clear promises about this, such as:

> I have made a covenant with my chosen one, I have sworn to David my servant, I will establish your line for ever and make your throne firm through all generations (Ps. 89:3–4).
>
> For the Lord has chosen Zion, he has desired it for his dwelling: This is my resting place for ever and ever; here I will sit enthroned (Ps. 132:13–14).
>
> This is what the Lord says, he who appoints the sun to shine by day, who decrees the moon and stars to shine by night, who stirs up the sea so that its waves roar – the Lord Almighty is his name: 'Only if these decrees vanish from my sight,' declares the Lord, 'will the descendants of Israel ever cease to be a nation before me' (Jer. 31: 35–36).

[18–20]

21. Forgiveness of sins is not only the basis on which we first enter the Church; it is also the basis upon which the Lord keeps us there. There would not be much point in receiving a pardon which had no further value. God's mercy would be futile and false if it was only given once. Every believer is conscious, throughout life, of many failings which need the mercy of the Lord. We could not stay in the Church for a single moment if we were not upheld by the constant grace of God in forgiveness. The Lord has called his people to eternal salvation, so they need to remember that pardon for sins is always available. If we belong to the body of the Church, our sins have been forgiven and are

daily forgiven through God's generosity, through the merits of Christ, by sanctification of the Spirit.
[22–28]

Chapter 2

Comparison of the false Church with the true.

1. I have tried to explain how important the ministry of the Word and sacraments should be to us, like a badge worn permanently to distinguish the Church. Where they exist, no mistakes or shortcomings should keep us from acknowledging the Church, and minor shortcomings do not invalidate this ministry. But when error forces its way into the citadel of true religion and essential doctrines are overturned, when the sacraments are abused, the Church inevitably dies, just as a man dies when his throat is cut. Paul makes this clear when he says, 'built on the foundation of the apostles and prophets, with Christ Jesus himself as the chief cornerstone' (Eph. 2:20). If the Church is founded on the teaching of apostles and prophets and through them believers are told to look for salvation in Christ alone, if that doctrine is shattered, the Church cannot continue to stand. The Church inevitably falls whenever essential doctrine gives way. If the true Church is 'the pillar and foundation of the truth' (1 Tim. 3:15), there can be no Church where lying and deception have taken over.

2. Since they have taken over under the papacy, we must understand its effect on the Church there. Instead of the ministry of the Word, a corrupt government exists, concocted from lies, which partly excludes God's pure light. In place of the Lord's Supper, there is awful sacrilege and the worship of God is distorted by a mass of intolerable superstitions. Doctrine, without which Christianity cannot exist, is buried and exploded; public services are hotbeds of

idolatry and profanity. Obviously when we refuse to take part in such wrong things, we run no risk of being cut off from the Church of Christ. Membership of the Church was not meant to be a chain to keep us in idolatry, sacrilege, ignorance of God and other evils, but rather to keep us in the fear of God and obedience of the truth.

Papists boast loudly about their Church as if there was no other, and make it clear that all who come out of the Church are schismatic and all who murmur against its doctrine are heretics. They try to prove their monopoly of the true Church by appealing to accounts of what once happened in Italy, France and Spain. They pretend to originate from those holy men who, by sound doctrine, founded and built up churches, established true teaching, and built the Church with their life-blood. They also pretend that the Church so consecrated by spiritual gifts and the blood of the martyrs was kept from destruction by a constant succession of bishops. They major on the importance which Irenaeus, Tertullian, Origen, Augustine and others attached to this succession. I must point out how empty these claims are, so that good men and lovers of truth may not be caught up in them. I would like to ask why these people do not quote Africa, Egypt and the whole of Asia. It must be because in these regions the sacred succession was broken, and it is by this they boast of having a continuous Church. So they fall back on the claim that they have the true Church because ever since it began it was never without bishops. They succeeded each other in an unbroken line. But what if I mention Greece? Why do they say that the Church died out among the Greeks, among whom there was an unbroken succession of bishops? They call the Greeks schismatics because they lost their privilege by turning away from Rome, the Apostolic See. Don't those who turn away from Christ deserve to lose their privilege even more?

The pretence of succession is futile, if succeeding generations do not keep the truth of Christ (which was handed

down to them by their fathers) safe and whole, continuing
to live by it.
[3–12]

Chapter 3

The teachers and ministers of the Church. (Their election and office.)

1. I am now going to speak of the Lord's pattern for Church
government.

It is obviously right that he alone should rule in the
Church and be seen to do so; its ordering should be administered by his Word alone. But because he does not live
among us physically (Matt. 26:11), to make his will clear
from his own lips, he uses the ministry of men, making
them his substitutes. He does not transfer his rights and
honour to them, but does his work through them, as any
workman would use a tool for his purpose.

I must repeat what I said before: God could have acted
without any human help, or could have worked through
angels, but there are several reasons why he chooses to use
men. First, in this way he displays his condescension to us,
by using us as his ambassadors to interpret his will to the
world, and to represent him. This is why we are called his
temples, since through our lips he speaks to men as from a
sanctuary. Second, it gives us a valuable training in humility as he expects us to obey his Word preached by people
like us (in some cases not as good as us!). If he himself
spoke from heaven, it would not be surprising if his solemn
Word was accepted reverently and immediately. Who
would not be in awe of his great power, bow down in the
presence of his great majesty and be overcome by his
amazing glory? But when an ordinary man of this world
speaks in the name of God, we prove our sincerity and
obedience by listening quietly to his servant, someone no
better than we are. God hides the treasure of his heavenly

wisdom in frail earthen vessels (2 Cor. 4:7) to test us. Also, nothing is more likely to produce mutual love than to bind men together in appointing one of them as pastor to teach the rest who are called to be disciples. If we were all self-sufficient, such is human pride, we would scorn others and they would scorn us.

So the Lord has bound his Church to what he knew would be the strongest bond of unity: he entrusted the doctrine of eternal life and salvation to men, for them to pass on to others. Paul was referring to this when he wrote to the Ephesians,

There is one body and one Spirit – just as you were called to one hope when you were called – one Lord, one faith, one baptism, one God and Father of all, who is over all and through all and in all. But to each one of us grace has been given as Christ apportioned it. This is why it says: 'When he ascended on high, he led captives in his train and gave gifts to men.' (What does 'he ascended' mean except that he also descended to the lower, earthly regions? He who descended is the very one who ascended higher than all the heavens, in order to fill the whole universe.) It was he who gave some to be apostles, some to be prophets, some to be evangelists, and some to be pastors and teachers, to prepare God's people for works of service, so that the body of Christ may be built up until we all reach unity in the faith and in the knowledge of the Son of God and become mature, attaining to the whole measure of the fulness of Christ. Then we will no longer be infants, tossed back and forth by the waves, and blown here and there by every wind of teaching and by the cunning and craftiness of men in their deceitful scheming. Instead, speaking the truth in love, we will in all things grow up into him who is the Head, that is, Christ. From him the whole body, joined and held together by every supporting ligament, grows and builds itself up in love, as each part does its work (Eph. 4:4–16).

2. In these words Paul shows that the ministry of men which God uses in ordering the Church is a vital bond to unite believers in one body. He also suggests that the Church cannot be protected without the guardians he has appointed. Christ 'ascended higher than all the heavens, in order to fill the whole universe' (Eph. 4:10). The way he works is this: he distributes his gifts to the Church through his ministers and so shows himself to be present there, by exerting the energy of his Spirit, and that he prevents it from becoming pointless and fruitless. In this way the saints are renewed and the body of Christ is edified. In this way we grow up in all things to him who is the Head and join with one another. In this way we are all brought into the unity of Christ, and so long as prophecy flourishes we welcome his servants and do not despise his doctrine. Whoever tries to get rid of this pattern of Church order or scorns it as of little importance, is plotting to ruin the Church. Even the sun's energy and essential food are not so necessary to the preservation of life as the apostolic and pastoral role is to the preservation of the Church on earth.

3. God has shown his approval on the office consistently by bestowing titles that make us regard it highly as one of our greatest blessings. He makes it clear that in raising up teachers he gives men a special privilege, when the prophet is made to exclaim, 'How beautiful on the mountains are the feet of those who bring good news, who proclaim peace' (Isa. 52:7), and when he calls the apostles the light of the world and the salt of the earth (Matt. 5:13–14). He could not praise the office more highly than when he said, 'He who listens to you listens to me; he who rejects you rejects me' (Luke 10:16).

But the most striking passage of all is in the second epistle to the Corinthians. He maintains that the ministry of the Gospel is the highest and most glorious aspect of the Church, because it communicates the Spirit of righteousness and eternal life (2 Cor. 4:6; 3:9).

These, and other references, should prevent people from belittling the ministry or allowing it to go by default. Again, there are examples in Scripture to teach us how necessary the ministry is. When God chose to bring the light of his truth to Cornelius, he sent an angel from heaven to send Peter to him (Acts 10:3). When he was pleased to call Paul to the knowledge of himself and graft him into the Church, he did not speak to him with his own voice, but sent a man to teach him about salvation and baptism (Acts 9:6–20)... It is not by accident that God entrusted these tasks to men. We must never despise the ministry which God made such a point of using.

[4–16]
[Chapters 4–11]

Chapter 12

Church discipline. (Its chief use in censures and excommunication.)

1. Now we must look briefly at the discipline of the Church. It depends to a large extent on the power of the keys and on spiritual authority. To make this clearer, we must divide the Church into two main groups – clergy and people. I use the term 'clergy' in the usual way, for those who carry out a public ministry in the Church.

We will deal first with the common discipline to which everyone must be subject, and then go on to the clergy, who have to be under a particular discipline as well. Some people hate discipline so much that they object to the very name, but we must remind them that no society or household can be controlled without it. It is even more necessary in the Church, which ought to be run in the best possible way. As the saving doctrine of Christ is the life of the Church, so discipline is like sinews which hold the parts together in the correct position. All who want to get rid of discipline will bring about the downfall of the Church. What would happen if everyone was allowed to do whatever he liked? As well as the preaching of the Gospel there must be private rebuke and correction to keep the teaching from being ineffective. Discipline is a curb to restrain those who attack the teachings of Christ, or a stimulus by which the uncommitted are challenged. Sometimes it can be a fatherly rod by which a believer who has sinned can be lovingly punished.

We can already see signs of chaos in the Church from lack of care and system in controlling members, so necessity alone demands a solution. The only solution is the one Christ lays down and good men have always accepted.

2. The first basis of discipline is private rebuke. If anyone does not do his duty willingly or behaves insolently, lives dishonestly or does anything wrong at all, he must be taken to task. We must all be willing to rebuke a brother when necessary. Pastors must be observant and not only preach to the people, but where necessary admonish them in their homes. Paul tells how he taught 'publicly and from house to house', claiming that he was 'innocent of the blood of all men' because he had declared 'all the counsel of God' (Acts 20:20, 26, 27). Doctrine acquires power and authority when a minister not only publicly declares what we owe to Christ but also has the right to demand that we should be obedient. If anyone deliberately refuses admonition or persists in sin, Christ's command is that, after he has been rebuked a second time in front of witnesses, he must be summoned to the judgment of the Church. The body of elders must correct him even more sharply, with public authority, so that if he respects the Church at all, he will submit and obey (Matt. 18:15, 17). If even then he is not humbled, but persists in evil ways, as a despiser of the Church, he must be banished from the company of believers.

3. The Saviour does not only speak of secret faults. We must look at the distinction between private and public sin. As to the former, Christ tells us to 'go and show him his fault, just between the two of you' (Matt. 18:15). As to the latter, Paul says to Timothy, 'Those who sin are to be rebuked publicly, so that the others may take warning' (1 Tim. 5:20). Jesus used the words 'If your brother sins against you' (Matt. 18:15). This must mean something only you know about. Paul followed his own injunction that those who sin openly should be rebuked openly, when he rebuked Peter publicly (Gal. 2:14). So the right course must always be to correct secret sins privately; but open sins, which create public scandal, should be dealt with by the Church.

4. Another distinction we must look at is that some sins are merely lapses and others are deliberate crimes. In correcting the latter, rebuke is called for, but also a sharp punishment. Paul illustrates this when he admonishes the incestuous Corinthian, and then punishes him by cutting him off from fellowship (1 Cor. 5:1–5). Perhaps now we begin to see how the spiritual judgment of the Church, which condemns sins according to God's Word, is the best support of sound doctrine, the best basis of order and the best bond of unity. When the Church expels from its fellowship the immoral, the dishonest and the disobedient, it is obeying the Lord's command. If anyone despises the judgment of the Church, the Lord makes it clear that he condemns himself and that this condemnation will be ratified in heaven. The Church is acting on the authority of the Lord when it condemns the obstinate sinner, and receives the penitent (Matt. 16:19; 18:18; John 20:23). Those who say that the Church can manage without discipline are wrong. The Lord himself saw that it would be necessary.

5. There are three good reasons why the Church must correct and even exclude people from fellowship. The first is so

that God may not be insulted by the term 'Christian' being used of those who lead corrupt lives, as if his holy Church were a conspiracy of wicked people (Eph. 5:25–26). The Church is the body of Christ (Col. 1:24) and cannot be defiled without disgracing Christ, her Head. So that nothing in the Church may bring disgrace on his sacred name, the erring member must be expelled. This is true too of the Lord's Supper, which would be spoiled by someone taking part wrongly. If the person leading the service knowingly admits an unworthy person, he is guilty of sacrilege. Chrysostom bitterly attacked priests who, from fear of the great, dared not refuse anyone ...

If this sacred mystery is not to be held up to scorn, discernment is needed in distributing it, backed by the authority of the Church.

The second purpose of discipline is so that good people may not be affected by regular contact with the wicked. We have such a tendency to go wrong anyway that bad examples soon lead us astray. The apostle referred to this when he told the Corinthians to expel the incestuous man from their fellowship: 'a little yeast works through the whole batch of dough,' he said (1 Cor. 5:6), and further commented, 'you must not associate with anyone who calls himself a brother but is sexually immoral or greedy, an idolater or a slanderer, a drunkard or a swindler. With such a man do not even eat' (1 Cor. 5:11).

A third result of discipline is that the sinner may feel ashamed and repent of his error. It is for our good that sin is punished: we become set in our ways if we are indulged, but feel convicted when punished. The apostle underlines this when he says, 'If anyone does not obey our instruction in this letter, take special note of him. Do not associate with him, in order that he may feel ashamed' (2 Thess. 3:14) and again when he says that he had handed the Corinthian over to Satan 'so that ... his spirit [may be] saved on the day of the Lord' (1 Cor. 5:5). He gave him over to temporal punishment so that he might be saved eternally. He gave

him over to Satan, because he is outside the Church, just as Christ is in the Church.
[6–28]
[Chapter 13]

Part XIV

THE SACRAMENTS

Chapter 14

The sacraments.

1. Alongside the preaching of the Gospel, the sacraments are a great strength to our faith. Clear doctrine is needed to explain why they were instituted and how they should be used. First, we must look at what a sacrament is. The simplest definition is that it is an outward sign by which the Lord assures us inwardly of his loving promises. This strengthens our faith so that we can prove our calling in his sight and before men. More briefly, a sacrament is God's witness to us of his favour towards us, by means of an outward sign. We in him confess our faith to him. Augustine defines a sacrament as a visible sign of a sacred thing, or a visible form of an invisible grace. But his definitions are too brief, which is why I have expanded them.
[2]

3. From these definitions, we can see that there cannot be a sacrament without a prior promise. The sacrament simply confirms the promise. God allows for our slowness and weakness and strengthens our faith in his Word. The truth of God is stable and sure, but our faith is feeble, so that unless it is supported on all sides, it is shaken and brought down. Our gracious Lord, with endless understanding, brings himself down to our level and by earthly means leads us to himself ...
[4]

5. We should not listen to people who argue that as we already either believe God's promises or we don't, the sacra-

ments teach us nothing. Either we already know what the sacrament teaches, or else we don't, in which case we must learn it from the Word. Our answer to that is that the seals which are fixed to diplomas and other documents are nothing in themselves and would have no purpose if nothing was written on the parchment. This does not prevent them from confirming and sealing the writing. Paul used the same illustration when he called circumcision a seal (Rom. 4:11). He maintains that Abraham's circumcision was not for justification, but was evidence of the covenant, through faith in which he had already been justified ... The sacraments make God's promises come alive to us, by presenting them in a pictorial, visible form ... Of course the believer does not stop short at the visible sign, but rises to the sublime mysteries which lie hidden in the sacraments.

6. The Lord calls his promises covenants (Gen. 6:18; 9:9; 17:2) and calls his sacraments signs of the covenants ... They are exercises which confirm our faith in the Word of God. God comes down to our physical level by giving us physical sacraments to lead us on. So Augustine calls a sacrament a 'visible word', because it represents the promises of God as in a picture, and puts them in our view. Another analogy is to call them pillars of our faith. Just as a building stands on its foundation, but is made more stable when supported by pillars, so faith leans on the Word of God as its foundation, but leans more firmly when the sacraments are added, as if supported by pillars. Or we could call them mirrors, in which we can glimpse the riches of God's grace.

7. It is irrational to argue that sacraments are not signs of God's grace toward us because they are taken by unbelievers also. Far from experiencing God's favour in this way, they only incur greater condemnation. But the same is true of the Gospel: by their argument the Gospel would not be a sign of God's grace because many spurn it. Similarly Christ himself would not be a sign of grace because many

who saw him did not receive him. We can be quite sure that the Lord offers us his mercy and a pledge of his grace, both in his Word and in the sacraments. But it can only be grasped by those who receive them with faith. Augustine referred to this when he said that the efficacy of the Word is produced in the sacrament not because it is spoken, but because it is believed ...
[8]

9. ... The sacraments can only fulfil their function when accompanied by the Spirit within, whose power alone can penetrate the heart and stir the emotions. If he is not active, the sacraments will be no more use than the sun shining on the eyes of the blind or sounds sent into the ears of the deaf. In distinguishing between the Spirit and the sacraments, his is the power and theirs the ministry. Their ministry without the work of the Spirit is empty and futile, but when he is at work in the heart, exerting his power, it is fully effective ...
[10–11]

12. ... We are not giving undue power to created things, but are saying that God uses those means that he sees fit to display his glory. As he feeds our bodies with food, lights us by the sun and warms us with fire, we know that these are only means of conveying his blessings. In the same way he feeds us spiritually by means of the sacraments. Their only work is to make his promises visible to us and to act as pledges of those promises. We do not put confidence in God's gifts themselves – they are a sign of God's blessing. Nor should our confidence be attached to the sacraments, but go beyond them, so that our faith can rise to the one who is the Author of the sacraments as well as everything else.

[13–16]

17. The sacraments have the same function as God's Word: they offer Christ to us, and in him, the treasures of grace.

They are useless if not received in faith just as wine and oil, when poured out, will go to waste unless they are poured into an open vessel. If the vessel is not open, it will remain empty even if the liquid is poured on to it. So we must not go along with some ancient Christian writers who have exalted the sacraments too highly. There is no special virtue inherent in the sacraments themselves. They cannot confer the gifts of the Holy Spirit upon us: they can only bear testimony to them. They cannot open our minds and hearts without the Holy Spirit's power. The sacraments are like messengers of good news. The Holy Spirit, whom the Lord gives to his own people, brings God's gifts along with him, gives a role to the sacraments and makes them profitable. God carries out what he has promised in the signs, and makes them effective ...

[18–26]

Chapter 15

Baptism.

1. Baptism is the sign of initiation by which we are admitted to the fellowship of the Church. In Christ we are accepted as children of God. He has given baptism to encourage our faith in him and also as a way of confessing it before others. Baptism is a sign of cleansing, that our sins have been completely wiped out and God will never refer to them again. It is his will that all who have believed should be baptised for the remission of sins. Those who see baptism only as confession of our faith have missed the main point. Baptism is tied to the promise of forgiveness. 'Whoever believes and is baptised will be saved' (Mark 16:16).

2. We understand this also from Paul's statements that 'Christ loved the church and gave himself up for her to make her holy, cleansing her by the washing with water

through the word' (Eph. 5:25–6), and again 'he saved us, not because of righteous things we had done, but because of his mercy. He saved us through the washing of rebirth and renewal by the Holy Spirit' (Titus 3:5). Peter also says that, 'baptism ... now saves you also' (1 Pet. 3:21). He did not mean to suggest that our salvation is perfected by water, or that water possesses in itself the quality of rebirth. Nor does he mean that baptism is the cause of salvation; only that certainty of it is received through this sacrament. The words used bear this out. Paul connects the Word of life and baptism of water: the message of washing from sin is proclaimed in the Gospel and then the message is sealed by baptism. Peter adds that it is 'not the removal of dirt from the body but the pledge of a good conscience towards God' (1 Pet. 3:21). The only purification which baptism promises is by the sprinkling of the blood of Christ, which is pictured as water because of the comparison with cleansing. How can anyone say that we are cleansed by the water itself, when it is only meant to bear testimony to the blood of Christ? ...

3. Baptism does not only cover the past sins. When we subsequently lapse, we don't have to look for a solution in other sacraments. Some people have delayed baptism until the end of their lives, so that they could be forgiven all that was past! We must realise that whenever we are baptised, we are washed and purified for the whole of life. Each time we sin we must remember that we were baptised for the forgiveness of sins. The purity of Christ is always effective and cannot be wiped out by our failure. Of course we must not assume that this is a licence for future sin: it is a tremendous consolation for those who are under deep conviction of sin, to keep them from despair. So Paul says that Christ was made a propitiation for us, for the remission of sins past (Rom. 3:25). But he does not mean to deny that forgiveness of sins is found in Christ for the whole of our life. God's mercy is afforded to all who, troubled by conscience, long

for a healer. Those who use it as a licence to continue in sin only provoke God's anger.

4. Many people believe that forgiveness, which we received when we were born again by baptism alone, is after baptism gained by penitence and the Church's power to forgive. This error arises because such people do not realise that baptism and the power to forgive are inextricably linked. The sinner receives forgiveness by the ministry of the Church, that is, the preaching of the Gospel. Through it we learn that we are washed from sin by the blood of Christ. Baptism is the symbol of this. Forgiveness is linked with baptism. The above error arises from the pseudo-sacrament of penance. Men love external things and so manufacture new props for themselves, as though baptism was not in itself the sacrament of penance. If repentance is called for through life, the power of baptism ought to last just as long! True believers when troubled by sin can always remember their baptism, and so be assured of eternal washing in the blood of Christ.

5. Another benefit of baptism is that it shows us our dying in Christ and new life in him. 'Or don't you know,' the apostle asks, 'that all of us who were baptised into Christ Jesus were baptised into his death? We were therefore buried with him through baptism into death' and that we 'may live a new life' (Rom. 6:3–4). By these words, Paul urges us to imitate Christ, reminding us that in baptism we are instructed, as Christ died, to die to our lusts, and as he rose, to rise to righteousness. He also takes the matter further when he says that Christ, by baptism, has made us partakers of his death, grafting us into it. As the twig gains nourishment from the root to which it is attached, so those who receive baptism with true faith, really know the efficacy of Christ's death in the mortification of their flesh, and the efficacy of his resurrection in the quickening of the Spirit. He bases his teaching on this, that if we are Christ-

ians we should be dead to sin and alive to righteousness. He uses the same argument when he writes that we are circumcised and put off the old man, after we are buried in Christ by baptism (Col. 2:12). In Titus 3:5 he calls it 'the washing of rebirth and renewal of the Holy Spirit'. First we are promised the free pardon of sins and the imputation of righteousness; second, the grace of the Holy Spirit, to form us again to newness of life.

6. The final advantage which our faith receives from baptism is that it assures us, not only that we are ingrafted into the death and life of Christ, but that we are so united to Christ himself as to be partakers of all his blessings. He consecrated and sanctified baptism in his own body (Matt. 3:13), so that in it he could have the strongest possible bond of union and fellowship with us. Paul even proves us to be the sons of God from the fact that we put on Christ in baptism (Gal. 3:27). It is understandable that the apostles are said to have baptised in the name of Christ, although they were instructed to baptise in the name of the Father and Spirit as well (Acts 8:16; 19:5; Matt. 28:19). All the divine gifts offered in baptism are found in Christ alone, but of course the one who baptises cannot help but invoke the name of the Father and Spirit also. We are cleansed by his blood, just because our gracious Father in his great mercy, wanting to accept us, made Christ the Mediator to bring about our reconciliation. We obtain new birth only from his death and resurrection when we are sanctified by his Spirit and imbued with a new and spiritual nature. So we find in the Father the cause, in the Son the matter, and in the Spirit the effect of our purification and new birth. First of all John and afterwards the apostles baptised with a baptism of repentance for the forgiveness of sins (Matt. 3:6, 11; Luke 3:16; John 3:23; 4:1; Acts 2:38, 41). By the term repentance, we understand regeneration and by forgiveness of sins, cleansing.

[7–13]

14. Now that it is clear what the Lord intended baptism to be, it is easy to see how it should be used and accepted. It is given to uplift, feed and strengthen our faith, so we are to receive it from the hand of its Author, being convinced that he himself is speaking to us in the sign. It is he who washes and purifies us, wiping out all memory of our faults. It is he who makes us partakers of his death, destroys the kingdom of Satan, subdues our desires and makes us one with himself so that, being clothed with him we can be reckoned as the children of God. We must be convinced of these things in our minds as surely as we see our bodies washed, and immersed in water. This is the surest guide to understanding the sacraments, that in physical things we are to discern the spiritual as if they were actually visible, since the Lord represents them to us by the signs. Nor does God simply let us watch an outward show: he leads us on to the actual object, and effectually carries out what is represented.

[15–22]

Chapter 16

Infant baptism. (How it accords with Christ's teaching and with the nature of baptism.)

[1]

2. We are agreed, then, that right understanding of signs does not lie in the outward ceremony but depends on the promise which it represents. If we want to grasp fully the effect of baptism, its object and real nature, we must not stop short at the outward act, but look forward to the divine promise offered in it, and rise to the mysteries represented. If we understand these, we have reached solid truth and the real meaning of baptism. We can then understand the nature and purpose of outward sprinkling … Scripture shows

that first of all it points to the cleansing from sin which we obtain by the blood of Christ, and second, to the mortification of the flesh. This consists in sharing in his death, by which we are born again to newness of life and so to the fellowship of Christ. It is also a sign to testify of our faith to men.

3. Before the institution of baptism, the people of God had circumcision in its place. The two signs resemble each other, but also have differences. When the Lord told Abraham to observe circumcision (Gen. 17:10), he promised that he would be a God to him and his seed. He also stated that in himself he was everything necessary to life, and that Abraham could count on him as a fountain of every blessing. These words include the promise of eternal life: our Saviour refers to immortality and the resurrection of believers when he says that 'He is not the God of the dead, but of the living' (Matt. 22:32; Luke 20:38). When Paul told the Ephesians of the great destruction from which the Lord had delivered them, because they had not been admitted to the covenant of circumcision, the implication must be that they were aliens from the covenant of promise, without God and without hope (Eph. 2:12). The first access to God and entrance to immortal life is the remission of sins. This corresponds to the promise of cleansing in baptism. The Lord covenanted with Abraham that he should walk before him in sincerity and purity of heart. This refers to putting to death or new birth. Moses explained this more clearly when he exhorted the people of Israel to circumcise the foreskin of their heart, because the Lord had chosen them for his own people, out of all the nations on earth (Deut. 10:15–16) ... A spiritual promise was given to the fathers in circumcision, similar to that given to us in baptism, since it illustrated the forgiveness of sins and the putting to death of the flesh. Christ, the source of both, is the foundation of baptism, so must also be the foundation of circumcision. He was promised to Abraham, and in him all nations are

blessed. To seal this grace, the sign of circumcision was added.

4. There is no problem in seeing how the two signs agree and how they differ. The promise, in which we have shown that the power of the sign consists, is the same in both – the promise of God's fatherly favour, forgiveness of sins and eternal life. The thing represented is the same also – new birth. The foundation on which the completion of these things depends, is identical. So, there is no difference in the inner meaning, by which the power and special nature of the sacrament is to be assessed. The only difference is in the external ceremony, which is the least important. The essential is the thing signified. So we may conclude that everything relevant to circumcision applies also to baptism, except, of course, the outward ceremony. The apostle tells us to bring every interpretation of Scripture to the analogy of faith (Rom. 12:3, 6). Certainly, in this instance, the truth is very clear. Circumcision was a kind of badge to the Jews, assuring them that they were adopted as the people and family of God and their first entrance into the Church, as they, in their turn, professed their allegiance to God. In the same way, we are initiated by baptism, to be counted among his people and to swear loyalty to his name. So it is incontrovertible that baptism has been substituted for circumcision, and serves the same purpose.

5. If we are to find out whether or not baptism should be given to infants, surely we would have to say that it would be stupid to confine ourselves to the element of water and the outward observance, and not allow our minds to rise to the spiritual mystery? Reason would tell us that baptism is rightly administered to babies. The Lord did not give circumcision long ago without making them (infants) partakers of everything represented by circumcision. He would have been deceiving his people with a sham, if he had reassured them with false signs. The very idea is shocking. He

distinctly states that the circumcision of the infant is the seal of covenant promise. If the covenant remains firm and un-moved, this is just as relevant to the children of Christians today as it was to the children of the Jews under the Old Testament. If they share the turning signified, how can they be denied the sign? ... The external sign is so linked in the sacrament with the Word that they cannot be separated. If they could, which would be the more valuable? Surely, when we recognise that the sign is subservient to the truth, we have to give it the lower place? The truth of baptism applies to infants, so why should we deny them the sign? The Lord himself formally admitted infants to his coven-ant, so what more do we need?

6. Scripture gives us an even clearer grasp of the truth. It is obvious that the covenant, which the Lord once made with Abraham, applies just as much to Christians now. We can-not imagine that Christ, by his coming, diminished the Father's grace. What blasphemy! The children of the Jews, when made heirs of the covenant, were separated from the heathen and called a holy seed, so the children of Christians (or those who have only one believing parent) are called holy, and differ from the unsanctified children of unbeliev-ers (1 Cor. 7:14). Since the Lord ordered his covenant with Abraham to be sealed in infants by an outward sacrament (Gen. 17:12), how can we say that Christians are not to do the same today, sealing the covenant in their children? ... Otherwise, if the testimony by which Jews were assured of the salvation of their children is taken from us, the result must be that, because of Christ's coming, the grace of God formerly given to the Jews, is less certain for us! We cannot say this without extreme insult to Christ, by whom the Father's love has been shed even more clearly on the earth. Surely we have to say that it cannot be more restricted and less obvious than under the dark shadows of the Law? [7–8]

9. Now we must see what benefits there are from the observance of baptism, both for believers who bring their children to church to be baptised and for the children themselves. We must never belittle the ordinance; the Lord rebukes those who dismiss everything they cannot grasp with natural understanding. The divine sign given to the child in baptism confirms the promise given to godly parents, and proclaims that the Lord is not only their God, but their children's. All this is to God's glory and increases the believer's love towards him, as they realise that his love is not only for them, but for their offspring. I am not convinced by the argument of some that the promise of salvation ought to be enough in itself. God obviously thinks otherwise! He knows our weakness and so tells those who claim the promise of mercy to their children to consider it their duty to offer them to the Church. There they are to be sealed with the symbol of mercy and so the confidence of the parents is strengthened as they see with their own eyes the covenant of the Lord physically imparted to their children. The children themselves derive direct benefit from their baptism when they are received into the Church and so become the greater interest to the other members. Also, when they grow up they are spurred on to serve God, who has already received them by the formal sign of adoption. We must take very seriously God's condemnation of those who despise the covenant symbol (Gen. 17:14). It is a rejection of offered grace.
[10–32]

Chapter 17

The Lord's Supper. (How it benefits us.)

1. After God has received us into his family, he does not look on us as servants but as sons. He himself is like a kindly and concerned parent who provides for our welfare

through the whole of life. Not content with this, he gives us a pledge to assure us of his unceasing generosity. Through his only begotten Son he gave another sacrament to the Church, a spiritual feast at which Christ proclaims that he himself is living bread on which our souls feed to receive eternal life (John 6:51).

Because of the importance of this sacred mystery, Satan has tried to deprive the Church of a precious sacrament. Long ago he introduced mists and darkness to obscure its light, and stirred up strife and argument to turn the simple from a desire for the sacred food. He has tried the same scheme in our own day. The signs, of course, are bread and wine which represent the invisible food which we receive from the body and blood of Christ. God, giving us new birth in baptism, grafts us into the fellowship of his Church and makes us his by adoption. He continues to act as a caring parent, providing the food which keeps us spiritually alive. Christ is the only food for our souls, and so our heavenly Father invites us to meet him so that, refreshed by communion, we may regularly gain new strength until we reach immortality in heaven. This mystery of the unseen union of Christ with believers cannot be naturally grasped, so God shows it clearly in visible terms. We realise that our souls are fed by Christ, just as the bodily life is sustained by bread and wine. Now we can understand the purpose of this mystical blessing: it assures us that the body of Christ was once sacrificed for us, so that we may now eat it and, eating, sense within ourselves the efficacy of that one sacrifice. We realise too that his blood was once shed for us, to be our perpetual drink. This is the point of Christ's promise, 'This is my body given for you' (Matt. 26:26; Mark 14:22; Luke 22:19; 1 Cor. 11:24). We are instructed to take and eat the body once offered for our salvation and as we see ourselves made partakers of it we can safely conclude that the power of his death will be efficacious in us. The covenant which he once consecrated by his blood is renewed and continued as confirmation of our faith every time he offers his blood to us as drink.

2. Godly believers derive great assurance and joy from this sacrament, as proof that they are part of the body of Christ, so that everything which is in him also belongs to them. It follows that we can confidently assure ourselves that eternal life, of which he himself is the heir, is ours, and that the kingdom of heaven into which he has entered can no more be taken from us than from him. We cannot be condemned for sin because he absolves us from guilt, having taken it on himself. This is the marvellous transaction he has made in his amazing goodness! Having become, like us, a son of man, he has made us, like him, sons of God. By his descent to earth, he has made possible our ascent to heaven. He received our mortality, and has given us his immortality. He took on our weakness, to make us strong in his strength. He submitted to our poverty and gave us his riches. He took on the burden of our unrighteousness which weighed us down, and clothed us with his righteousness.

3. The sacrament of communion bears witness to all these things, enabling us to understand that they are revealed to us as surely as if Christ was physically present with us, to be seen and touched. These are words which can never lie nor deceive – Take, eat and drink. This is my body which is given for you: this is my blood, which is poured out for the forgiveness of sins. In telling us to take, he makes it clear it is ours. In telling us to eat, he makes it clear that it becomes part of us. In stating that his body was given and his blood poured out, he shows that he laid them down, not for his own advantage, but for our salvation. We must grasp that the heart of the sacraments is in these words: it is given for you; it is poured out for you. The distribution of the elements would be meaningless, if his body and blood had not been given for our redemption. So they are represented by bread and wine, to indicate that they are intended to nourish our spiritual life. As bread sustains our bodies, so

the body of Christ is the only food to keep our souls alive. When we see wine held out as a symbol of blood, we must compare its use to the body with what is spiritually given by the blood of Christ. It refreshes, strengthens and exhilarates. So the bread broken and the wine outpoured accurately represent what is communicated to us by his body and blood.

4. The chief object of the sacrament is to seal and confirm his promise by which he testifies that his flesh is our food and his blood our drink, feeding us to eternal life. He is the bread of life and whoever eats it shall live for ever. Thus the sacrament sends us to the cross of Christ, where that promise was carried out perfectly. We cannot eat Christ aright unless we see the efficacy of his death. When he called himself the bread of life, he referred to his being given to us as a partaker of our human mortality and making us partakers of his immortality. When he offered himself in sacrifice, he took our curse upon himself to cover us with his blessing. By his death he swallowed up death and in his resurrection he raised our corruptible flesh, which he had assumed, to glory and incorruption.

5. The final issue is that this must all become ours in actuality. This is done through the Gospel and more clearly by the Lord's Supper, where he offers himself to us with all his blessings and we receive him by faith. The sacrament, of course, does not make Christ become the bread of life for the first time. It reminds us that we may always feed on him and gives us the desire to do so. It assures us that whatever Christ suffered was to give us life, and that this quickening is eternal. Christ could not have been the bread of life to us if he had not been born, if he had not died and risen again. So he could not be the bread of life to us today if the results of his birth, death and resurrection were not eternal. Christ himself expressed this in his own words: 'The bread that I will give is my flesh, which I will give for the life of the

world' (John 6:51) ...

Two faults must be avoided here. We must not think too little of the signs, separating them from their meaning; nor must we think too much of them, which can obscure the true mystery. There is some disagreement about the way we partake of Christ. Some say that eating Christ's flesh and drinking his blood are nothing more than believing in Christ himself. But Christ himself seems to have gone further. He says that as we eat and drink, we truly partake of him. It is not simply knowledge of him. It is not the sight of the bread, but eating it which nourishes. In the same way the soul must partake of Christ in reality, so that by his energy it may grow spiritually. To the first group mentioned to eat is merely to believe, while I hold that we eat Christ's flesh by believing, that eating is the effect or fruit of faith. For them eating is faith, whereas I would say it is the consequence of faith. The difference seems small put in words, but it is great in truth. Although the apostle teaches that Christ dwells in our hearts by faith (Eph. 3:17), no one could take that dwelling to be faith itself. We can see that it explains the wonderful effect of faith – because of it, believers have Christ living in them. In the same way, Christ chose to call himself the bread of life (John 6:51), not only to teach that our salvation is treasured up in the faith of his death and resurrection, but also, because of real communion with him, his life passes to us and becomes ours, just as bread gives strength to the body.
[6–9]

10. So our conclusion must be that the body and blood of Christ feed our souls, just as bread and wine support our bodily life. There would be no point in the signs, if our souls did not find their nourishment in Christ. This can only be because Christ is made one with us and refreshes us by the eating of his flesh and the drinking of his blood. Although it seems an incredible thing that the flesh of Christ, so far removed physically, should be food to us, we have to re-

member the immense inward power of the Holy Spirit and
how stupid it is to try to measure its immensity by our feeble
efforts. What our minds cannot grasp, faith must engender
– that the Spirit really does unite things separated by space.
Christ transfuses his life into us by that sacred communion
of flesh and blood, just as if it entered our very bones and
marrow. He seals this truth in the Lord's Supper, not by
giving an empty sign, but by displaying the power of the
Spirit by which he fulfils what he has promised. That which
the bread and wine signify is presented and offered to all
who partake. It is received only by true believers who accept it with genuine faith and heartfelt gratitude. This is
why the apostle said: 'Is not the cup of thanksgiving for
which we give thanks a participation in the blood of Christ?
And is not the bread that we break a participation in the
body of Christ?' (1 Cor. 10:16). There is no reason to say
that this expression is figurative, giving the sign the name of
the thing signified. I agree, of course, that the breaking of
the bread is a sign, not the reality, but having said this, we
rightly infer from the display of the sign, that the thing itself
is displayed. Unless we accuse God of fraud, we can never
say that he offers an empty sign. If by the breaking of bread,
the Lord truly represents the partaking of his body, there
can be no doubt that he imparts the reality too. We must always remember that the truth of the thing signified is also
present. The Lord puts the symbol of his body into your
hands to assure you that you truly partake of him. It gives
us such assurance to know that the visible sign is given as
the seal of an invisible gift.

11. I believe what the Church has always believed, that the
sacred mystery of the Lord's Supper consists of two things
– the physical signs and the spiritual truth. There is the
thing meant, the matter which depends on it, and the effec-
tiveness of both. The thing meant consists in the promises
which are included in the sign. By the matter I mean Christ,
with his death and resurrection. By the effect, I mean

redemption, justification, sanctification, eternal life and all the other benefits Christ bestows on us. When I say that Christ is received by faith, I do not mean only by intellect and imagination. He is offered by the promises, not for us to stop short at mere sight or knowledge of him, but so that we may enjoy true communion with him. Then the other blessings follow ... The Lord's Supper proclaims first that we may become one body with him, and second, that we may experience the result of this as we share in all his blessings.

31. Those who believe that Christ's flesh is not present unless it is in the bread are greatly mistaken. They do not allow for the secret working of the Spirit, which unites Christ himself to us. Christ does not seem to them to be present, unless he descends to us, although we can just as well come into his presence when he raises us to himself. The quibble is over the process: they place Christ in the bread while we consider it wrong to bring him down from heaven. You must judge for yourself. But never subscribe to the falsehood that Christ is not present in the Supper if he is not secreted under a covering of bread. We speak of a heavenly mystery and it is not necessary to bring Christ down to earth for us to be united with him.

32. If anyone asks me about the process, I do not mind admitting that it is too high a mystery for my mind to grasp or my words to express. I feel rather than understand it. I can rest safely in the truth of God and embrace it without question. He declares that his flesh is the food, his blood the drink for my soul. I give my soul to him to be fed with such food. In the Lord's Supper, he bids me take, eat and drink his body and blood under the sign of bread and wine. I have no doubt that he will truly give and I receive ... Such is the bodily presence which the nature of the sacrament requires. It is shown in such power and efficacy that it not only gives our minds absolute assurance of eternal life, but also

secures the immortality of our bodies quickened by his immortal body. Some teach the mixture or transfusion of the flesh of Christ with our soul, but I repudiate this. It is enough for us that Christ, from the substance of his flesh, breathes life into our souls. He diffuses his own life into us, though the real flesh of Christ does not enter us. There can be no doubt that the analogy of faith by which Paul commands us to test every interpretation of Scripture (Rom. 12:3) clearly agrees. If anyone opposes such a clear truth, they must examine their own faith ...

[33–50]

[Chapters 18–20]